Delivering Successful PMOs

Peter would like to thank his wife, Lisa, and all of his family for the support that they have shown in him pursuing his writing and speaking career.

Ray would like to dedicate this book to his wonderful wife, Jennifer, for the years of happiness and support.

Delivering Successful PMOs

How to Design and Deliver the Best Project Management Office for your Business

PETER TAYLOR

and

RAY MEAD

GOWER

Published by
Gower Publishing Limited
Wey Court East
Union Road
Farnham
Surrey, GU9 7PT
England

Gower Publishing Company
Suite 420
101 Cherry Street
Burlington
VT 05401-4405
USA

www.gowerpublishing.com

Peter Taylor and Ray Mead have asserted their right under the Copyright, Designs and Patents Act, 1988, to be identified as the authors of this work.

British Library Cataloguing in Publication Data
A catalogue record for this book is available from the British Library.

Library of Congress Cataloging-in-Publication Data
Taylor, Peter, 1957-
  Delivering successful PMOs : how to design and deliver the best project management office for your business / by Peter Taylor and Ray Mead.
    pages cm
  Includes bibliographical references and index.
  ISBN 978-1-4724-1379-6 (hbk) -- ISBN 978-1-4724-1380-2 (ebook) --
  ISBN 978-1-4724-1381-9 (epub) 1. Project management. I. Mead, Ray. II.
Title.
  HD69.P75T3953 2015
  658.4'04--dc23

2015010129

ISBN 9781472413796 (hbk)
ISBN 9781472413802 (ebk – PDF)
ISBN 9781472413819 (ebk – ePUB)

MIX
Paper from
responsible sources
FSC
www.fsc.org   FSC® C013985

Printed in the United Kingdom by Henry Ling Limited, at the Dorset Press, Dorchester, DT1 1HD

Contents

List of Figures

List of Tables

About the Authors

Ray Mead

Ray Mead is the founder and CEO of p3m global, a specialist project, programme and portfolio management consultancy.

Ray has 18 years of project management experience gained across many different industries and in many different countries, including extended or frequent stays in Spain, Germany, China, Australia and Saudi Arabia.

He has a BA (Hons) in French, Spanish and Marketing from Southampton University and studied his MBA at Surrey in partnership with Jiaotong University in Beijing.

Prior to becoming involved in consultancy he worked as a project manager in the telecommunications industry and also had spells in training and education.

In 2005 Ray started the EMEA operations of PM-Partners group and has worked internationally with his clients, building an effective team, business model and ethos that would eventually become the foundation for p3m global.

Outside work, Ray lives in Southampton with his wife Jennifer, has a moderate obsession with Southampton FC and the England rugby and cricket teams, and is the Conservative member for Shirley on Southampton City Council.

Peter Taylor

Peter Taylor is the author of two best-selling books on 'Productive Laziness' – *The Lazy Winner* and *The Lazy Project Manager*.

In the last three years he has focused on writing and lecturing, with over 200 presentations around the world in over 25 countries and with new books out including *The Lazy Project Manager and the*

Project from Hell, *Strategies for Project Sponsorship*, *Leading Successful PMOs*, and *The Thirty-Six Stratagems: A Modern Interpretation of a Strategy Classic* – with a number of other book projects currently underway.

He has been described as 'perhaps the most entertaining and inspiring speaker in the project management world today' and he also acts as an independent consultant working with some of the major organisations in the world coaching executive sponsors, PMO leaders and project managers.

His mission is to teach as many people as possible that it is achievable to 'work smarter and not harder' and to still gain success in the battle of the work/ life balance.

More information can be found through his free podcasts on iTunes and at:

- www.thelazyprojectmanager.com

Peter can be reached at peter.b.taylor@btinternet.com and is available for:

- keynote presentations and lectures;
- master of ceremonies;
- inspirational workshops;
- coaching;
- authoring.

Foreword

STUART DIXON

When I started out in the field of PMO 20 years ago, it wasn't even called a PMO; the first one was a KPI department, and then we became a Project Office. Over the intervening years I think I have been in an office which has used all variants of the title of PMO. In Peter's last book on the subject of PMOs – *Leading Successful PMOs* – he explained what was meant by the term PMO and showed what can be achieved by a successful PMO.

From the last book the question that I was left asking, which is the same one that is asked time and again on the various online forums, is 'How do I get a successful PMO in my organisation?'. There is a plethora of papers on the subject of PMOs, some of which provide advice on how to set up a PMO, and others which show how many PMOs fail within the first few years. So it seems as if anyone could follow one of those guides on how to set one up, but are you going to set up something that will last and will actually fulfil what the organisation is expecting of it?

This book explains in simple terms how to set up a PMO that will not only last the duration, but deliver a real, measurable difference to the organisation. What differentiates a PMO from a truly successful PMO is the ability to make a step change in the way the organisation implements projects and programmes. Following the steps detailed in this book will allow a PMO leader to deliver something that will last and will be aligned to the goals of the organisation.

Being a PMO leader requires a special kind of person who has charisma, influence, tenacity and an understanding of just how empowering a PMO can be to the organisation. The leader of a successful PMO is one who wants to make a difference to his or her organisation. This book will provide you with the inspiration and guidance to do both.

With the combination of the right person to make it happen and this book I am looking forward to more successful and long-lasting PMOs taking themselves and their organisations to the next level.

About Stuart Dixon

Stuart Dixon is the current Secretary of the APM PMOSIG (and ex-Chairman)[1] – the UK's only specialist interest group for all PMO practitioners. Through regular conferences, newsletters, blogs and via the LinkedIn group the APM PMOSIG is a great starting place for anybody leading or working in a PMO to share ideas, network and become professionally engaged.

---

1 See www.apm.org.uk/group/apm-pmo-specific-interest-group

Acknowledgements

Peter Taylor would like to thank all of those who have read and appreciated the first book, *Leading Successful PMOs*, and all who have attended and contributed to the one-day workshop based on that book that has been delivered around the world. Your enthusiasm and input has been inspirational and has encouraged him to take this next step on the PMO 'journey'.

Peter would also like to thank his co-author Ray for joining in this endeavour to guide even more organisations to the successful delivery of their PMOs.

Ray Mead would like to thank everyone he has worked with at PM-Partners and p3m global, be they clients, colleagues or partners, for the contribution their efforts and interactions have made to the way we see the world.

Special thanks to Issam Houdane, partner and friend, for the shared experiences that inspired this book and the invaluable collaborations to conceive and perfect the PAD3T™ model.

Ray would also like to thank his co-author Peter for the encouragement to work on this project and for sharing his experience to make it the digestible volume you now hold.

Both authors would like to thank Jonathan Norman of Gower Publishing for helping promote the value of PMOs through good leadership and great delivery.

Introduction

Delivering Successful PMOs is intended to be the companion book to *Leading Successful PMOs* (Gower) by Peter Taylor, which was a guide to all project-based organisations providing a common language to describe the variety of possible PMOs, explaining how to do the right things, in the right way, in the right order, with the right team, and identifying what made a good PMO leader.

Delivering Successful PMOs takes this to the next level and the authors, Peter Taylor and Ray Mead, aim to provide readers with a clear framework to conceive, design, build, prove and embody an enterprise PMO inside an organisation, dealing with the strategic intentions, the politics, the people and the projects.

This is not a book about delivering PMOs. Many organisations have implemented PMOs and they have built them in many different shapes and sizes and with varying levels of effectiveness. This is a book about delivering *successful* PMOs; that is, PMOs that are built to last.

The first thing to say is that it is far from easy and, depending on your current levels of maturity, usually means a fundamental reorganisation of your business and potentially reaching outside your own organisation to gain some help along the way. Noses will be put out of joint, empires will be crushed and there will be much weeping and gnashing of teeth at the water cooler.

When it's done correctly, though, it is worth it. A successful PMO brings and consistently creates real, measurable value for your business, so, if you've got the will, the wherewithal and a strong sponsor behind you this book will give you steps to follow to design and deliver a *successful* PMO.

Let the games begin.

> **❝** By three methods we may learn wisdom: first, by reflection, which is noblest; second, by imitation, which is easiest; and third by experience, which is the bitterest. **❞**

> Confucius

CHAPTER 1
A Short Reflection

What is it with all the acronyms?

And why do they all start with P?

A full and frank discussion on the various different meanings and roles of the PMO can be found in Peter's precursor to this book, *Leading Successful PMOs*. For those who have not yet had the good fortune to read that particular book, we'll summarise again for you here.

As you can imagine, knowing what kind of PMO you need and want has a dramatic impact on how you deliver it, which we will be discussing further in later chapters.

'PMO' is an androgynous term – my understanding of a PMO is not the same as your understanding of a PMO. Nor is it the same as your boss's understanding or your CEO's, or your customers', or even your PMO manager's understanding. The truth is that there are many different types and functions of a PMO and it can be built to serve different purposes. The challenge is having those functions clearly defined and uniformly perceived in the business. When this doesn't happen things start to unravel fairly quickly, as we will explore shortly.

On paper, PMO stands for 'Project Management Office'. It sounds physical; you can just imagine a bustling room with people running about frantically, phones going and with Gantt charts and network diagrams plastered all over the walls. The reality is often very different. A PMO can also be 'virtual': it can be dispersed over several locations; in smaller organisations it can even be half of one person's time.

Confusingly, PMO can also mean Programme Management Office or Portfolio Management Office, again depending on its function. People have sought to sometimes differentiate their PMO by calling it different things: P3O (for Portfolio, Programme and Project Office), PSO (Project Support Office), PDO (Project Delivery Office), PCO (Project Control Office), CPO (Central Project Office), CP3MO (you get the idea ...).

We have yet to come across a C3PO, but if any readers know of any, the authors would be delighted to hear about it and we strongly reject the suggestion that PMO can sometimes stand for 'Projects Mostly Over-budget'.

To save confusion, we will retain the term PMO and take that to mean an office which, depending on its maturity and the need it fulfils, can perform a multitude of different functions.

As stated in the preceding book *Leading Successful PMOs*:

> *The Project Management Office (PMO) in a business or professional enterprise is the department or group that defines and maintains the standards of the business processes, generally related to project management. The PMO strives to standardise and introduce economies of repetition in the execution of projects. The PMO is the source of documentation, guidance and metrics on the practice of project management and execution.*
>
> *A good PMO will base project management principles on accepted, industry standard methodologies, as well as government regulatory requirements as applicable. Organisations around the globe are defining, borrowing and collecting best practices in process and project management and are increasingly assigning the PMO to exert overall influence and evolution of thought to continual organisational improvement.*
>
> *Establishing a PMO group is not a short term strategy to lower costs. Recent surveys indicate that the longer organisations have an operating PMO group the better the results achieved to accomplish project goals. (which might lead to eventually lowering costs)*
>
> *PMOs may take other functions beyond standards and methodology, and participate in Strategic Project Management either as facilitator or actively as owner of the Portfolio Management process. Tasks may include Monitoring and Reporting on active projects (following up project until completion), and reporting progress to top management for strategic decisions on what projects to continue or cancel.*

That was the long explanation; in simpler, shorter terms a PMO was described as:

Doing the right things, in the right way, in the right order, with the right team.

Whilst *Leading Successful PMOs* explored what was meant by a PMO and what a PMO could deliver to a business that invested in a PMO or collection of PMOs, and what made the new breed of PMO leader successful, this book explores the mechanics of good delivery of a PMO, once the purpose was understood.

The framework given in this book was designed as a comprehensive method to deliver an Enterprise PMO, but it can be equally adjusted, scaled and applied to the delivery of any type of PMO. The authors will discuss the critical sizing of a PMO later on and reflect that it does matter when it comes to a PMO.

❝ It is in the nature of the human being to seek a justification for his actions. **❞**

Aleksandr Solzhenitsyn

CHAPTER 2
A Further Justification

Mark A. Langley, President and CEO of the Project Management Institute stated in the PMI's 'Pulse of the Profession™ 2013: The High Cost of Low Performance' that:

> *Failed projects waste an organisation's money: for every US$1 billion spent on a failed project, US$135 million is lost forever ... unrecoverable.*

The report later went on to confirm what we all believe:

> *The best performing organisations approach project, program and portfolio management differently from their peers:*
>
> 1. *They create efficiencies to drive organisational success.*
>
> 2. *They focus on talent management and improving its role in project management.*
>
> 3. *They employ project, program and portfolio management practices strategically.*

And it is the authors' belief that the best custodian for all of this key activity is an effective and well designed, well executed and well managed PMO.

The challenge for businesses these days is pretty clear: multiple stakeholders, increasing complexity of projects and an expanding range of scope, faster time to market, more flexible strategic planning and execution all have contributed to making project management a tough task for C level executives.

Again, it is beholden of the PMO as the single point of management and execution for this increasing (in scale and complexity) project-based activity to aid the C level executives in this key area.

The good news is that, as the PMI's Pulse of the Profession™ 2013 goes on to say:

> The percentage of organisations with project management offices (PMOs), or a similar centralized project management department, is increasing. Nearly seven out of 10 organisations (69 per cent) have a PMO, up from six out of 10 (61 per cent) in 2006, when PMI first began tracking this.

Excellent growth and on a path perhaps to all organisations coming to the state of appreciation for what a PMO could do for them and their organisation (the emphasis being on the 'could'). The report continues:

> Organisations are increasingly establishing PMOs with enterprise-wide responsibilities, which are growing more rapidly than those that serve a department, region or division of the organisation. Compared to their department-specific, regional and divisional peers, enterprise-wide PMOs are more focused on strategic aspects of project management, such as training, portfolio management, establishing metrics, and developing core project management maturity. These findings suggest that as more enterprise-wide PMOs are created, more projects will be aligned with the business goals of the organisation, and project management will be executed more strategically.

Again, excellent news from PMI, and not only from PMI either, the 2012 KPMG report – *Business Unusual: Managing Projects as Usual* – speaks of the PMO as being an 'enabler':

> As organisations grow and are involved in multiple projects, the key requirement is to translate the best practices across projects to bring efficiency in the way things are managed. The strategies undertaken to ensure effective execution of the project, plays a key role in project success. The role of the PMO is of great importance as it is looked upon as a key enabler within organisations to assist and build key strategies. PMO also intervenes to ensure conflicts are resolved and dealt with in a systematic manner and engage with useful project management tools such as communication, budgeting and planning which leads to a project success.

KPMG note that:

Organisations have started investing in a big way on multiple initiatives simultaneously. The increase in number of stakeholders, each with their own style of project management, has led to the increased risk of missing out on basics of project management excellence. The 'PMO concept' is not new to the industry. With projects in many organisations becoming global, involving multiple business units and locations, the benefits of PMO are more visible.

Almost 64 per cent of the survey respondents to this survey identified the PMO as a means to optimise on quality and on scope, time and budgetary constraints. But the report continues with a word of caution:

The benefits of the PMO are widely known, however in order to achieve the expected benefits, PMO needs to be implemented with defined processes, tools and governance mechanism. Having an effective PMO can help in bringing efficiency to the overall project management. Learning from past projects can be identified, documented and used to the benefit of future projects by the PMO. Also allowing a dedicated team to monitor the project heath at periodic intervals can help the project team to focus on project execution.

But it does seem, cautionary note aside, that the PMO can have a positive impact on project maturity inside and organisation and in delivering greater project success. And KPMG further state that:

The progressive development of the organisation's project management approach, methodology, strategy and decision-making process are dependent on having a dedicated entity for project management.

And concludes with this:

It is observed from our study that organisations having a project management office are at a considerable advantage as the PMO plays a positive role and impacts the project management maturity.

But it is not just any PMO that delivers to a business at this level; the move towards Enterprise PMOs as we saw from PMI's Pulse of the Profession™ 2013 is significant.

PWC in their report 'Insights and Trends: Current Portfolio, Programme, and Project Management Practices' declare that 'Increasingly, successful organisations employ PM to drive change and achieve their business objectives' and more to the 'PMO' point 'Established project management offices result in projects with higher quality and business benefits'.

PWC continues with this insight:

> *With the exception of the smallest scale portfolios, the portfolio performance levels of respondents whose [Portfolio Management] programs are managed by an Enterprise PMO are consistently higher than those whose portfolios are managed by other groups or individuals, resulting in an increased likelihood of portfolios that meet schedule, scope, quality, budget, and business benefits requirements.*

PWC actually declare that a PMO being established is one of the key criteria to an organisation achieving Level 4 maturity on their PM maturity model (you can read lot more about such maturity models in the appendices).

So 'all in all' this is good news for the 'PMO' world and the potential of this relatively new business unit.

It seems that most agree that a well-designed and well established PMO can deliver projects at a higher quality level and more attuned to the real and current business benefits.

Which brings us neatly to 'delivering' such a 'successful PMO'.

" Whatever needs to be maintained through force is doomed. "

Henry Miller

CHAPTER 3
Destined to Fail? ...

Whisper it in hushed tones, but the PMO may already be an endangered species.

The sheer scale of PMO implementation in the last 5 years has invariably led to numerous botched attempts to deliver them. The authors themselves know of several organisations who have abandoned the idea of implementing their PMO or have even dismantled a PMO that had been running for several years.

The ESI report from 2015, *The Global State of the PMO*, identified that some 72 per cent of respondents reported that the value of their PMO was questioned in some way by key stakeholders and inevitably some of these 'questions' were translated in to 'cancellation' of the PMO.

In each case there is one central theme: the PMO failed to deliver and/or failed to demonstrate value.

Part of the issue here is that it is generally accepted that the idea of a PMO as a good thing is on the 'up', that is to say it is becoming increasingly common for PMOs to exist inside organisations – the *State of the PMO 2014* (PM Solutions) identifies an increase from 48 per cent in 2000 to 80 per cent (90 per cent in large firms), having PMOs in place, and notes 'Growth in the number of PMOs reflects their rising importance to companies'.

So it would seem that a bright shiny new PMO could be on the shopping list for a lot of executives but this 'rush' to secure their very own PMO is causing some of the issues and failures as there is insufficient knowledge and experience in the marketplace to support all of these PMO initiatives.

The PMO, in the wrong hands, quickly develops a bit of an image problem. Project managers end up seeing it as the 'project police' enforcing the use of standards, forms and templates that add little value to the projects that they are working on. It becomes all too unbalanced, too much about process and not enough about people and certainly not about value. In these cases the PMO may enforce the use of tools which replicate information already recorded into other tools; it may slow down projects by insisting on end-stage reviews where little happens (apart from a lot of effort on the part of project managers and a seemingly endless delay to the project itself) and where lessons are never seemingly learned.

Conversely in this situation, the business ends up seeing the PMO as an irrelevant overhead, impeding the business rather than empowering it. A luxury item at best that seems to want more and more money for 'improvement initiatives' to dam the ever-rising tide of project failure.

The attitude, quite legitimately, is 'projects are still failing, so why do we have this PMO anyway?'

In both cases the PMO has failed to deliver and/or demonstrate value – value to the business and value to the people it supports.

A recent article published by the Cranfield School of Management (author is not noted) on the subject of PMOs declared some startling facts about PMOs:

> Our research shows that around 70% of large organisations have some form of PMO. But our research also shows that, whilst some can be shown to contribute to increased project and programme success rates, others are less effective. Overall, it appears organisations have a PMO for one or more of the following reasons:
>
> 1. To reduce the risk of projects failing to deliver to time, cost and quality targets
>
> 2. To increase the success of projects and programmes in delivering the business value expected
>
> 3. To make more efficient use of project resources by using a 'shared service'
>
> 4. To make more effective use of scarce skills and resources across projects and programmes'

Points 2 ('increase success') and 3 ('efficient use') are pretty positive reasons for having a PMO but points 1 ('reduce the risk') and 4 ('effective use of scarce resources') are less than positive approaches and could well lead to perceived PMO 'failures'. The demand by an organisation to make the most of insufficient resources is pretty much a recipe for failure at some point.

The report notes intriguingly:

Our study of nearly 150 organisations, of which 70% had PMOs, showed that, overall, those organisations with PMOs did not have higher project success rates, but somewhat counter-intuitively, they had lower levels of management satisfaction with the level of project performance and value delivered.

Now this may well be due to the fact that the PMO is in its early stages and is dealing with the 'negative' aspects of the work that it is expected to do; it takes time to move on to the 'positive' aspects that really matter. I always say that if your PMO is (a) the project police and (b) the company project firefighter then you will fail – sooner rather than later!

There is nothing wrong with being the project firefighter as long as your PMO is the right sort of firefighter – not the sort that rushes around with siren blaring and battling fires but the sort that spends most of their time (as do professional firefighters) in preventing fires from happening in the first place!

Perhaps some insight can be gained as to why some, or a lot, of PMOs are not seen to be really delivering significant value from the PM-Partners: PMO Trends 2012 report where it is suggested that:

The value of a PMO does not lie in the number of processes it has established but in how much it contributes to the improved delivery of projects and the organisational benefits derived from projects.

And the Cranfield report touches on another one of the key themes in *Leading Successful PMOs*, uniqueness:

Research shows that few PMOs are stable: as issues evolve, business circumstances change and the PMO achieves some or all of its objectives, its purpose and role need to be reappraised and its services and resources adapted to remain effective or developed to meet new challenges that emerge.

" Strive not to be a success, but rather to be of value. "

Albert Einstein

CHAPTER 4

... Or Designed to Succeed?

Success, the authors believe, needs to be planned up front, needs to be built into the PMO model and needs to be part and parcel of the delivery of that PMO into the recipient sponsoring organisation.

There must be a strong and clear business case for the PMO to exist – the fact that 'a bright shiny new PMO' could be on the shopping list for a lot of executives is not a business case.

There has to be clarity of the investment required to deliver the right (and successful) PMO into the business.

A realistic appreciation of the time to plan, start-up, set-up, operate, and transfer the PMO into the very fabric of the organisation is a mandatory pre-requisite.

Linked to all of this there must be strong sponsorship for the PMO – and that means one with both authority and commitment to the PMO cause.

And there has to be a plan. We all know the maxim: if you fail to plan then you are planning to fail, and for a PMO this is particularly relevant. But there is a critical issue with regards to this.

You need a plan developed by someone who knows how to truly deliver a successful PMO! And let's be honest here; such people, right here, right now, are few and far between – the 'PMO' concept is just too new.

When *Leading Successful PMOs* was researched Peter struggled to find 100 job advertisements for PMO leaders around the world; today it would be relatively easy to find 100 such openings for PMO leaders in the UK alone – all this in the short space of five years.

Now during this time has there been a massive programme of development of PMO leaders? Have hundreds of PMOs matured to the point of releasing their managers into the marketplace? Has each PMO been an unmitigated success? Have we reached the pinnacle of PMO knowledge?

Of course not – it is still early days for most organisations and early days for most leaders of PMOs.

As such the authors of this book aim to help and guide those that are planning a PMO or struggling to deploy one effectively with a framework for success.

And if you need some more help on the way then they are only an email or call away.

" Stay committed to your decisions, but stay flexible in your approach. **"**

Tony Robbin

CHAPTER 5
Introduction to the Plan

Delivering a PMO is a project. Well actually, if done properly and certainly for a PMO of any significant size, design and delivery of such a PMO is more like a programme, but trying to run a programme in a low maturity environment is vaguely akin to trying to orchestrate a symphony when nobody can play the instruments yet. The key here is to approach the whole process with the right mindset and so thinking of it as a project instils the basics and is a good starting point.

So as a project, it should have clear deliverables, well defined stakeholders and sufficient allocated resources.

Moreover, it should be a model project, approached with the same degree of rigour and professionalism that will be expected from all the projects in its future care. It should be the shining light, the standard by which all other projects are measured and the platform for many future project successes.

At p3m global[1] (p3m global specialises in project, programme and portfolio management delivery and capability development), when we run PMO delivery projects we are particularly at pains to ensure the project is managed very tightly. After all, what moral authority would we have as a project management consultancy if we couldn't manage our own projects properly? The same goes with managing your PMO delivery project. Nobody will take the PMO seriously if the project that delivered it was a shambles.

The first Project Management Office (PMO) is understood to have been established in the early 1980s by the US Army, leveraging the concept of the war room to oversee major programmes and operations. In the 1990s the requirements of events such as Y2K created a growing need for the PMO.

Although today many Project Management Offices exist, it is important to recognise:

- The introduction of a PMO is a significant organisational change – implementation will need to be carefully planned in alignment with your organisation's culture.

---

1   See www.p3m.global

- Significant benefits can be realised through consistency and efficiency.
- There is no universal definition of a PMO – so the PMO function, role and service must be defined individually for each individual organisation.
- It is vital to review the PMO regularly as it needs to adapt and change with the business.

The primary steps for a successful PMO delivery are:

1. Establish an Improvement Forum for Project Management, made up of influential people from all major functions of the business.
2. Develop a PMO Charter to define and agree the value proposition to the business, what the PMO will do, the services it will offer and the customers it will provide the services to. Identify key stakeholders, an executive sponsor and obtain sign off. Define the build phase that will be required to set up the PMO and its associated processes.
3. Conduct a current and future state assessment to help define the work ahead and provide some measurement of success as you move forward.
4. Establish the PMO using a project management approach with a formal business case and scope ensuring that outcomes are realistic and achievable within the constraints of the business and culture.

There is a strong link between the length of time a PMO has been operating and project success rates: the longer the better. While 37 per cent of those who have had a PMO for less than one year reported increased success rates, those with a PMO operating for more than four years reported a 65 per cent increase in success rates. As with all business improvement projects there is a cost and a payback, only by considering this can you determine if it is a worthwhile investment.

Regardless, the first step is to define the terms of reference and the scope of the project management office for your organisation.

And aligned to this is the management of expectations as to what and how quickly a PMO will deliver results.

Every project has a life cycle and with all this in mind p3m global have developed a standard life cycle for all PMO delivery projects.

This life cycle framework is known as PAD3T™ and a visual representation of this can be seen in Figure 5.1.

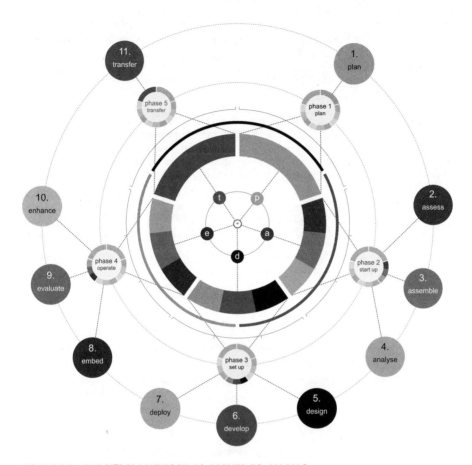

FIGURE 5.1   PAD3T™ FRAMEWORK AS APPLIED TO AN PMO

The PAD3T™ life cycle has 5 phases which are made up of a total of 11 stages (hence the name, P + (3 'A's + 3 'D's + 3 'E's) + T). It is a proven approach to the design, implementation and optimisation of P3M improvement initiatives, including PMOs, that is the product of our own expertise and experience but also incorporates the best of the fields of maturity modelling and continuous improvement. It is built to be both comprehensive and flexible, appropriating existing good organisational practice into customised initiatives across the three key development streams of people, process and technology that we have already discussed. Not all phases or stages are necessary but they are executed according to the individual needs of the organisation. The steps are loosely summarised thus:

P   Plan   Each time p3m global approach this type of consulting engagement it is usually treated as a change programme but if you are not used to working in a benefits-led environment it can be implemented as a project and therefore more deliverable based. The emphasis here is the capturing of a vision of what needs to be achieved and the main outcomes and benefits you want to gain from it.

A   Assess   The Assess stage looks to benchmark the current state and performance of the organisation's people, its processes and the use of its tools and technology. This is achieved through a combination of online perception analysis surveys, one-on-one structured interviews and facilitated workshops with key stakeholders. Existing practices are assessed and the output from this phase is a clear 'As-Is' Report

A   Assemble   This is essentially a requirements gathering phase where all stakeholder requirements are captured in detail and assembled into a 'To-Be' desired state.

A   Analyse   In this stage a gap-analysis is performed on the information collected in the previous two stages and begin to establish a new blueprint or 'target operating model' for the future PMO capability, along with a roadmap of how to achieve it.

D   Design   Once the blueprint has been accepted in principle, the final and more detailed design is put together, including how to ensure that the new processes integrate seamlessly and effectively into the existing project management systems or mapping out how and when the new technology will be configured to empower the business process and how to engage staff along the way.

D   Develop   In this stage any manuals are written and the tools and templates, business process workflows, etc., are all produced.

D   Deploy   In this stage the initial methodology training would be performed and/or the tool would be installed and configured according to the business processes. Initial champions and change agents would be trained and empowered.

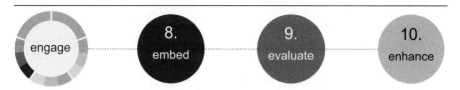

E Embed   In this stage the methodology and/or tool is embedded into the organisation through training of a wider base of people. As well as this, depending on requirements, other initiatives may be executed such as internal marketing of the new systems. Coaching and mentoring programmes may also be initiated.

E Evaluate   In some cases, p3m global clients require us to run the new systems for them for a specified period of time. During this period, p3m global would monitor the performance of key, pre-agreed metrics, gauge the level of benefit realisation and evaluate the performance of the new systems

E Enhance   Based on the outcome of the performance metrics and of the general feedback of users, p3m global would then implement a series of targeted improvements to the systems to 'fine-tune' them to ensure total fitness for purpose. This becomes an essential part of any maturity 'continuous improvement' initiative.

T Transfer   When the organisation is ready to assume full accountability, the new systems are transferred to its ownership through a controlled series of steps, after which, a review of the whole programme and its benefits is performed.

It should be noted that the entire PAD3T™ life cycle may not be necessary. You can make use of any assessment data or reviews the organisation has already undertaken, for example. This is discussed and scoped in the Plan phase along with the number of necessary stages required and the degree of detail required. The general approach is to keep the level of engagement proportionate to the business need and the benefit opportunity identified.

CHAPTER 6
Phase 1 – Plan PMO

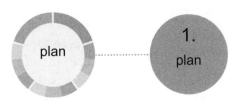

FIGURE 6.1 PHASE 1

Designing and building a PMO can be a daunting exercise. There are many things to consider as we can see in Table 6.1 and if this job has landed on your desk the natural question would be 'Where do you start?' but a more appropriate question might be 'Why are we doing this?'

TABLE 6.1 PLAN PHASE

OBJECTIVES	KEY ACTIVITIES	BENEFITS
• Align the various stakeholders of the PMO Programme in a clearly defined and understood direction	• Mobilise resources • Organisation chart • Develop project charter • Develop detailed scope of work • Address risks and issues • Develop detailed programme work plan • Develop quality plan • Conduct Kick-off presentation	• Clear project objectives • Clear understanding of responsibilities • Programme resource allocation • Seamless programme progress

Plan

Like any project, it should be undertaken for a clear reason and it should operate within an organisational context; what are the desired outcomes we want to achieve? How is this going to improve the business? How can we measure that

.provement? As we saw in the previous chapter, the PMO has to demonstrate value to the business in order to survive. And so it is important to define what that value is as early as possible and use it as the main driver of the project and measurement of success.

As an example PMO implementations can provide such ROI (return on investment) through cost savings by:

- Project Resources: More efficient resource allocation and priority setting. The organisation gains clearer visibility of resource needs for all projects which allows the allocation of resources with more effect, usually through a portfolio management process.
- Improving Project Health: PMOs can provide methodology standards or guidelines, training and certification for project managers, knowledge sharing through lessons learned and other effectivity gains as well a critical 'quality' assurance service to ensure overall project health improvements.
- Managing the Portfolio: PMOs can oversee the full project investment for an organisation and make recommendations on project relevance to strategy, which should be challenged or even halted, which should be accelerated and the overall health of the project portfolio.

As *Leading Successful PMOs* states with regard to this subject:

> *Any business case should focus on and define the key problems that the solution should address. In this case it is the investment in a PMO. For any change to take place and be supported there has to be either a 'pain' that needs resolving or a benefit that wants to be achieved – or perhaps a combination of both. For the PMO the 'pain' will be a list of project issues, low quality of deliverables, late delivery, budget overruns and so on. The benefit might include avoiding lost opportunities or for accelerating strategic deployment.*

It further suggests some ideas for business benefits of a PMO:

> – *Improved efficiency: through standardization of operations and methods*
>
> – *Higher utilization: through better resource allocation and capacity planning.*

- *Accurate time to ROI: through faster and better quality project status reporting. (progress, risks, issues, changes etc)*

- *Improved project initiation: through a more realistic prioritization of project work*

- *Better decision making: through the combining of business 'silos' into one business representation*

- *Raised professionalism: through the development of a project management community*

p3m global speak of the 'Value of a PMO':

- *Maintains 'big picture' understanding of all business change*

- *Ensures right programmes and projects are launched, consistency of delivery, things done well the first time*

- *Provides assurance, consistency, mentoring and single source reporting function*

- *Provides a view across the organisation and aggregates resources and risk and can anticipate what can go wrong*

- *Improves organisational accountability, decision-making, transparency and visibility*

- *Protects revenue and spend, enhancing value for money*

- *Facilitates change more effectively and efficiently*

- *Improves organisational programme and project delivery*

- *Protects reputation and stakeholder confidence*

Once the reasons and justifications for the PMO (project) have been identified and agreed, they should be enshrined in a project charter, like any other project and that should be produced and circulated by the Project Sponsor.

Having an appropriate Sponsor, i.e. one with authority and commitment to the cause, should not be underestimated. It is crucial and the project will fail without it. The authors have walked away from PMO implementations where there was no clear sponsorship; rather that than be associated with a failed project.

For further reading on good project sponsorship you may be interested in *Strategies for Project Sponsorship* (Management Concepts Press) by Peter Taylor, Vicki James and Ron Rosenhead.

The PM-Partners: PMO Trends 2012 report covers this very point:

> *When executives support the PMO, success rates improve significantly along with maturity. However, a strong executive sponsor is required to guide the PMO and stay aligned with the business.*

It is important at this stage, through the charter or through any other appropriate method, for the sponsor to announce and publicly back the project. There should be a clear communication of what is happening and why; of what the benefits to the business will be, including the project management community itself.

The danger at this stage is that the project is perceived as 'just another management fad'. If people think the project is a flash in the pan or if they are unclear about what it will achieve or how it will affect them they will not be bought in which will result in a much more difficult implementation.

If the sponsor has clearly articulated the benefits of the project and made it clear that the stakeholders will be listened to and that they will have the opportunity to input and contribute to the finished product this will significantly improve the way the project is received.

So who would be the appropriate sponsor for a PMO deployment? A sponsor should have the profile and authority to command respect for the project but should also be actively engaged and committed to the project on a week-to-week basis. If we are delivering an Enterprise PMO, the sponsor should be C-suite level – The highest-level executives are usually called 'C-level' or part of the 'C-suite' referring to the 3-letter initials starting with 'C' and ending with 'O' (for 'Chief XXX Officer'); the most common 4 such officers are Chief Executive Officer (CEO), Chief Operations Officer (COO), Chief Financial Officer (CFO) and Chief Information Officer (CIO).

An Enterprise PMO is a significant and permanent function of the business, handling all transformational activity. It is therefore only right that a senior executive of the company takes ownership of the initiative. In the case of a departmental PMO, such as a PMO for the IT function of the business then the sponsor should be the head of department, in this case the IT Director or similar.

Once the sponsor has announced the project then it is up to the project manager to begin planning the project. Like any project, the scope of what is to be delivered needs to be clear. There will not be 100 per cent clarity at this stage because we have yet to assess the current situation and perform any gap analysis or even gather any detailed requirements. This will all come as the project progressively elaborates through its phases. By the time we reach the 'D' phase we will have absolute clarity on exactly what we are delivering. For now, though, we can mobilise our team, establish project governance and control systems and we can produce a scope, a work breakdown structure and an initial version of the schedule.

Each work package should have its own plan, complete with scope, success criteria, associated risks, RACI matrix (this describes the participation by various roles in completing tasks or deliverables for a project or business process. It is especially useful in clarifying roles and responsibilities in cross-functional/departmental projects and processes. RACI is an acronym that was derived from the four key responsibilities most typically used: Responsible, Accountable, Consulted, and Informed), etc. These Work Package Plans can be produced now and refined at a later stage. The important thing is that the deliverables of each work package are documented and agreed now so the expectations are clear about what is being delivered as part of this project (and what is not).

The output of the Plan phase should be a documented project management plan. This will include the scope document and the WBS but also all the other main components one would expect. Achieving accuracy on the schedule and budget will be challenging as this project is not a repeatable one and it likely that many people involved in it have not undertaken anything similar. The time and effort it takes to produce the deliverables in the work packages will vary substantially from organisation to organisation, depending on what functionality is being delivered, how quickly decisions are made (and then followed through and stuck to) as well as how involved senior stakeholders want to be and how much process and governance is already in existence. Project Managers should allow for these Enterprise Environment Factors when estimating but, as a guide, the budget should be accurate to at least Budget Estimate level (–10 per cent to +25 per cent). Stakeholders should be made aware that, as each stage is planned and executed, planning accuracy ranges should narrow to Definitive Estimates (–5 per cent to +10 per cent) for each work package.

And now a quick word on resources.

Again, this will vary with the scale of your task so, rather than speak about the types and quantities of resources you will need it may be better to think about the range of skills you will need. Clearly, project management skills are needed to manage this project but the project manager does not necessarily need to be an expert themselves in all facets of portfolio, programme and project management. Like all industries, though 'technical' skills are an advantage, they do not preclude somebody from inherently being a good project manager. Project managers in any industry can succeed because of their drive, clarity of thinking and ability to engage wide ranges of stakeholders, including the subject matter experts who can provide the technical expertise.

As well as project management skills you will need, particularly in the first phases of the project, assessment skills and business analysis skills. The first 'A' phase of the project is all about this and requires a thorough benchmarking to be done on the current P3M environment. Then you will need to run detailed requirements gathering workshops and try to get to the bottom of the key organisational issues which are impeding successful project delivery. Many of these sessions will be at a senior level, especially when discussing portfolio and programme management, so you will need people detailed enough to extract and develop specific requirements who are also comfortable facilitating and operating at board level.

Later in the project you will need technical writers to document processes and procedures in a clear, unambiguous way. You will also need knowledge of project management tools and the ability to map the functionality of each tool to the requirements of the business, as well as the technical ability to install and configure them. You will also need marketing and change management skills. A large part of this project is making these substantial changes work in the business. They need to be understood, accepted and, ideally, embraced by the P3M community and to achieve this you will need to employ a wide range of change management techniques which will be discussed as we progress through the stages.

Outputs from Phase 1

The following are the typical outputs from the initial phase of this framework:

- Business Case.
- PMO Project Charter.
- Project Team Organisation Chart.
- RACI Matrix.
- Baseline project scope.
- Risks and Issues.
- PMO Project KPIs.
- Go/No Go Presentation.

CHAPTER 7

Phase 2 – Start Up PMO (A Phase)

FIGURE 7.1   PHASE 2

Any major transformation exercise starts with a look at 'where are we now?' – a consideration of the 'As-Is' situation with a view to the future state, the 'To-Be' desire which can be seen in Table 7.1.

TABLE 7.1   START UP PHASE (A PHASE)

OBJECTIVES	KEY ACTIVITIES	BENEFITS
• Assess the current PM competency, processes and tools and understand the real drivers for change using OPM3 and PM-Pulse™ as a guide • Capture the new future PM state by gathering client requirements	• Competency assessment • Project management tools assessment • Stakeholder requirements analysis • P3M requirements gathering • Gap analysis between the current state and the future state • Examine PM common needs and requirements across the various departments	• Provides full visibility of overall competency and capability in your people across all project roles • Align skills strategically with the organisation's project portfolio • Provides a basis for performance management for project managers, from directors • Clear definition of target state (to-be) • Stakeholders are engaged and aligned

Assess

When regarding an organisation's P3M capabilities (Portfolio, Programme and Project Management) the approach should be no different. By understanding the current landscape we can begin to target and prioritise our improvements. More importantly, a well-conceived assessment allows us to provide a set of baseline metrics with which to chart our progress and the value we are bringing to the business.

There are many ways of assessing the current Portfolio, Programme and Project Management capabilities of the organisation, the most widespread and accepted frameworks being project management maturity models. More details of the most common ones can be found in the appendices.

Even though they are powerful models giving the ability to benchmark against international standards and a framework for improvement, project management maturity models are not the only assessment vehicles to use. They are heavily skewed towards the processes of the organisation and offer

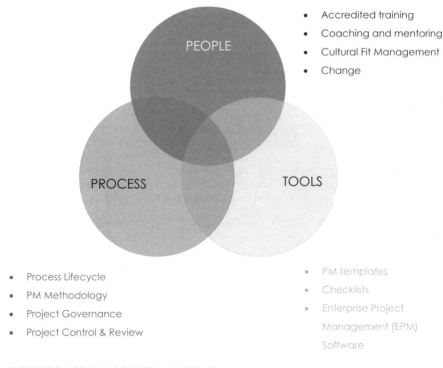

- Accredited training
- Coaching and mentoring
- Cultural Fit Management
- Change

- Process Lifecycle
- PM Methodology
- Project Governance
- Project Control & Review

- PM templates
- Checklists
- Enterprise Project Management (EPM) Software

FIGURE 7.2 PEOPLE, PROCESS AND TOOLS

relatively little guidance on asking, beyond whether a process exists and is used, is it actually effective and fit for purpose? The other area maturity models do not assess is the competency of the people in the Project, Programme and Portfolio Management community.

An organisation can have the finest and most complete set of processes but if the calibre of their people is not up to scratch, or if they have not trained them so that they acquire the necessary skills for their role then the organisation will never fully succeed. Organisational capability comes from having the right mix of people, processes and tools – see Figure 7.2 on the previous page.

PEOPLE

In *The Talent Management Handbook* (Berger and Berger, 2003) Lyle Spencer defines a competency as 'a reliably measurable, relatively enduring characteristic (or combination of characteristics) of a person, team or organisation, which causes and statistically predicts a criterion level of performance'.

Moreover, it is generally accepted that competency is a combination of three main factors of Knowledge, Skills and Attitudes (KSAs) and that this combination alone leads to being successful in any given role.

The PMI® Competency Framework (Figure 7.3) concurs, defining competence as:

"The demonstrated ability to perform activities within a project environment that lead to outcomes based on defined and accepted standards ... Competent project managers consistently *apply* their project management knowledge and personal behaviours to increase the likelihood of delivering projects that meet the stakeholders' requirements. Project managers bring together their *knowledge, skills, personal characteristics and attitudes* when focusing on delivering a project."

FIGURE 7.3 PMI COMPETENCY FRAMEWORK

For example, a project manager may have good interpersonal skills but may not be competent to join an organisation unless he or she displays the right knowledge and behaviours. Singing is a skill, whereas yodelling is a competency;

writing is a skill, but being ambidextrous is a competency. The difference is where and how the skill is applied.

Similarly, an individual may have a deep appreciation of the nuances of golf but can be found sorely wanting when invited to apply that knowledge on the fourth tee.

Individuals are *competent* in what they do when they know the technical details of a given subject and can apply this in practice, displaying the right attitudes and behaviours to continue to do this consistently in any given situation (e.g. when under pressure or in adverse or hostile conditions).

PMI® have recognised this when developing their own Project Manager Competency Development Framework. The framework is based broadly on the KSA concept and transposes these factors into three dimensions of project manager competence:

- Knowledge Competencies: What the project manager knows about the topic of project management.
- Performance Competencies: How the project manager *applies* project knowledge to project activities in a live environment.
- Personal Competencies: How the project manager *behaves* when performing activities within the project environment.

Over and above these dimensions, PMI® suggests two other dimensions to obtain a truly complete picture of competency in a job role:

- Industry Specific Competencies: In some industries there may be specific knowledge, skills or attitudes that are needed to succeed therein. In the ICT industry this may take the shape of technical knowledge of IP protocols or telecommunications infrastructure.
- Organisational Competencies: There may be specific elements of the organisation in which a project manager works that, when mastered, enables them to perform better. This may be the ability to use certain systems, methods, escalation paths and other organisational process assets. It may also involve a deep appreciation of the political or decision-making environment.

The 'Industry Specific' and 'Organisational' competency domains, though important in a fully balanced competency appraisal, are not within the scope of a best-practice standard and so it is left to each organisation to choose whether to include them in any assessment of competency.

In his definition of competency, Spencer qualifies what he means by 'reliably measurable' as meaning that 'two or more independent observers or methods (tests, surveys) agree statistically a person demonstrates a competency characteristic'.

BENEFITS OF COMPETENCY ASSESSMENTS

Competency assessment has long demonstrated value to organisations in areas such as recruitment and selection, performance management, employee development, succession planning and organisational change.

Competency assessments allow organisations to identify the essential knowledge required alongside professional and personal characteristics for high performance in a given job role. They help leaders identify desired behaviours and compare them to actual behaviours exhibited on the job. An effective competency assessment should encompass a holistic approach when reviewing an employee, including the measurement of knowledge, performance, personal competencies, industry specific awareness and organisational understanding.

There are certain clear benefits of the competency framework for an organisation:

- A common understanding of critical success factors and desired behaviours within the organisation.
- Integration of organisational process to competencies helps the interpretation of big picture concerns in day to day working.
- Better management and effective decisions regarding cost intensive processes like selection, hiring and promotions.
- Assessment, feedback and communication regarding performance becomes standardised thus facilitating a common culture.

Using competency assessments can also provide a reality check and baseline of individual performance. Beyond a simple recognition of skill levels, strengths that emerge from the competency assessment can be used to determine readiness for a promotion or justification for new, more challenging learning opportunities. By confirming their aptitudes and skills, individuals can make decisions that reinforce their favoured career path, give them confidence in their next career move, and keep them from getting stuck in their current position.

It is important to note that the benefits obtained from using competency assessments are not just restricted to organisational level. Individual benefits can also be derived from the process such as:

- identifying individual strengths and weaknesses;
- providing evidence for needed developmental activities;
- increasing ongoing dialogue with the boss;
- fostering continuous improvement;
- informing short- and long-term career decisions.

LIMITATIONS OF ONLY ASSESSING KNOWLEDGE

Traditional assessment is limited to testing knowledge and skills, for example in an interview or in a formal written paper. Whilst these methods undoubtedly have their place, it is possible to have knowledge of a particular skill or ability, and be able to discuss or answer questions in great detail, but be completely incapable of actually performing the task being described.

For example, consider the ability to drive a Formula 1 racing car. Many followers of the sport can describe at great length exactly what is needed in order to drive such a car, even being able to describe the individual challenges likely to be faced, and how to overcome them. However, put them behind the wheel of such a car and ask them to actually drive it, and it is extremely unlikely they will even be able to even engage a gear.

So it can clearly be seen that it is essential that capability – and not just knowledge – be assessed. When we conduct assessments, we achieve this by conducting workshops using either tailor-made scenarios (i.e. built-in collaboration with our client), or existing generic scenarios, and using those to assess the employee actually performing the task being reviewed. In conjunction with traditional assessment methods, this allows the full spectrum of reporting, including capability.

The Role of the Assessment Sponsor

The role of the Assessment Sponsor is a crucial one as it is the link between the assessor and those to be assessed within the organisation. We have learned from our previous experiences that the way in which the assessment process is first presented to those to be assessed and the explanation of the reasons for it will define the quality of data captured in the assessment.

It is key that the assessment process is presented in a positive light by the Assessment Sponsor, highlighting the fact that the process is designed to enable the organisation to invest in its Project Management personnel based on a clear baseline understanding of skills and competencies.

This introduction is also an excellent opportunity for the Assessment Sponsor to give candidates a clear understanding of the corporate goals of such an undertaking, as well as explaining the benefits which will be recognised by both the individuals and the business.

The assessment process must be portrayed as an opportunity for the project management community, not a threat. The Assessment Sponsor must clearly articulate this not just at the initiation stage of the assessment but consistently throughout the process.

The quality of the output from the assessment is only as good as the quality of the information provided by those being assessed therefore full engagement, driven by the Assessment Sponsor is a must. Again, lessons learned from previous assessments have taught us to increase the emphasis on this role.

Tools

Just as organisations often make the mistake of investing in generic training to try to improve their project performance, the same mistakes are made with regard to project management tools. Because tools are tangible and because software now provides the answer in so many aspects of modern life many organisations believe that investing in an enterprise project management tool will be the answer to their problems. They are important and, when configured correctly, can dramatically improve access to decision-making information. Like generic training, however, the problem occurs when tools are seen as an isolated, catch-all solution.

In most modern organisations it is likely that project managers are using several different tools for different purposes. Usually, there may be a system in which the project is allocated to them, usually linked to some kind of billing system. There may then be a tool to manage and store their documents, like Sharepoint; they may then have another system for building their schedule (such as Microsoft Project) and another for building their actions, tasks and risk registers (Microsoft Office); there may then be a separate system for logging their time and so on and so forth.

When assessing the tools aspect of an organisation it is best to use a three-step approach:

1.   Through a series of interviews, capture and list all the different tools in use across the project life cycle (even if they are not designed for project management purposes. Some tools may be implemented and owned by Finance, for example, but they impact the project manager's time and capture data relevant to the effective management of the project).

2.   Gather information on which elements of functionality are being used in each tool versus those elements that are not being used. For example, project managers may only be using the scheduling functionality of Microsoft Project and not the resource utilisation functionality.

3.   Map the functionality of each existing tool being used to the potential functionality of it that is not being used. Then, by comparing the active and latent functionality across the tool base it is possible to begin to identify efficiencies where some tools can be eliminated and their functionality can be picked up by other tools already in use.

Project Interfaces

One final component of the Assess stage is to analyse the 'touch points' that a typical project has with the rest of the organisation throughout its life cycle. Most modern organisations operate some kind of matrix structure when it comes to project management. That is to say projects occur 'horizontally' across the organisation, using shared resources from various different operational functions as their skills are needed. It is not only important to understand how projects interact with operational functions (for example, how a project would request resources and allocate them work) but also how the project interacts with the organisation's support functions.

Very often it is possible to improve the processes of the project management function itself but the real cause of project failure may be outside the control of that function; very often it lies with the fundamental manner that the organisation deals with projects in its generic business processes. How the organisation's Finance function requires its projects function to spend, budget and report financial information will have a profound effect on how the projects are conducted. Similarly, restrictions imposed by an organisation's procurement function can limit accessibility to skills and expertise while the way a project is serviced and supported by the organisation's IT function will affect the means of communication and information storage it can employ.

Throughout the course of its life cycle a project will typically require services, support, decisions, guidance and resources from its performing organisation. Identifying improvements in how this works may end up being the key to not just having a PMO that works well in isolation, but actually delivers seamless change as an integrated part of the overall organisation.

In summary, the purpose of the Assess stage is to understand and benchmark the current level of the organisation's P3M capability. This is broadly achieved by looking at the maturity of the organisation's processes against international standards like OPM3 (The Organisational Project Management Maturity Model or OPM3® is a globally recognised standard for assessing and developing capabilities in Portfolio Management, Programme Management, and Project Management), the knowledge, skills and behaviours of the organisation's people (and therefore their competency) and the functionality being used across the organisation's tool base.

The results of these assessments then need to be consolidated into a report which would form the main deliverable of the stage. Crucially this should contain key benchmarked metrics so that, once the PMO has been in operation for some time the performance of the organisation can be compared against the current situation. These will be built upon in the next two stages and will form the 'As-is' metrics of the Gap Analysis deliverable in the Analyse stage.

Assemble

The heart of the Assemble stage is gathering requirements for the future PMO. It involves visualising a 'desired state' for the future and distilling this desire into specific, tangible requirements. Not all of the requirements will be possible in the final solution but the key aspect of this stage is to capture as much as possible from as diverse a stakeholder pool as possible so that the requirements can later be analysed, consolidated and prioritised for implementation in later stages.

The Assess stage left us with a clear picture of the current state; the 'As-Is', and when the assessment interviews are taking place it's very important at that stage not to drift conversations into how things *should* work. However, now in the Assemble stage we are specifically asking these questions to try to define a 'To-Be' environment. Now the discussions will focus around how things could and should be better and the desired outcomes needed for the organisation to deliver its projects and programmes more efficiently and effectively.

Depending on the scope for your PMO project you will need to determine sets of requirements for project level, programme level and portfolio level and will need to engage different groups of stakeholders according to their interests and perspectives of the initiative. Whichever way you choose it is important that this process is 'sold' well to the P3M community; if the Assess stage was their chance to show what *doesn't* work, the Assemble stage is their chance to input into how things *should* work. It is a crucial part of change management and if the right stakeholders are not involved now then it will be an uphill task to encourage adoption of the governance standards you build later down the line.

A good approach would be to run a series of workshops and interviews with specific groups of stakeholders at various levels of the organisation. The approach should be a comprehensive one, covering a similarly broad range of stakeholders as the Assess stage. Groups of project managers should be represented, as should functional managers who supply the organisation's projects with resources. Customers of the project management processes should be represented, as should people who currently commission projects. Following on from the project interface assessment from the Assess stage, specific workshops should also be set up with the organisation's support functions (HR, Finance, IT, Procurement, etc.) to determine their expectations and requirements for how projects and programmes will interact with them in the future. For example, how will resources be allocated to projects? How will people be appraised for project activities? How much budgetary responsibility will project managers have? How will project managers budget for risk? All these questions and more will need to be put to the organisation's support functions. Their opinion is not the final word as it is the PMO project manager's job to balance all requirements with best practice and to make informed and engaged recommendations. It is, however, important that all groups have had an opportunity to have their say and to demonstrate how things should work from their own perspective.

There will need to be engagement for senior directors and executives as well, especially when determining requirements for the programme and portfolio functions. For these senior stakeholders it is often better to conduct one-to-one interviews. This creates an environment where the stakeholder can be frank about what the organisation ought to be doing and has the added bonus of being able to come straight to the point, rather than tiptoeing around the perceptions of other stakeholders in a workshop environment.

One problem you may experience may be who to include in workshops and who to interview. There are several generic criteria to determine whether an executive is appropriate for interview:

- Are they knowledgeable about how the business areas in question operate?
- Do they have projects and/or programmes under their direct responsibility?
- Are they empowered to define and implement strategy for a given business unit?
- Do they have a clear vision of the way forward and how they would like it to be?
- Do they support the aims of the PMO project?

Following on from the final point, it is obviously preferable that they support the aims of the project. However, these interviews are sometimes particularly good for stakeholders who could be seen as indifferent or even hostile to the project, as by elevating them to the status of a senior stakeholder you are sending the message that their opinion is valid and respected.

It is generally advisable that there is a good deal of preparation before these interviews. Senior executives may also have contributed to the Assess stage and will therefore expect the PMO project manager to be familiar with certain elements of the organisation, such as the way strategy is formulated and disseminated into business unit plans.

The essential thing is not to waste their time and it may help to obtain an audio recording of the conversation so you or other members of your team do not need to keep coming back to them asking for the same information. In general the kind of questions you want to ask will be:

- What are the aims and objectives for their part of the business?
- What are the key performance indicators that they are measured on?
- What do they expect from the new PMO and how can it make their lives easier?
- What concerns do they have about the PMO? Do they see any risks and issues with the project?
- How would they like to be involved?

In general, you should stick to open questions to encourage coherent thoughts and opinions, resorting to closed questions only when you require clear clarification on a point or to obtain a definite yes or no on a given subject.

Note, in an environment that has never had a PMO before or has suffered from a poorly performing PMO it may be necessary to hold a series of awareness briefings prior to these interviews and workshops. If people understand the basic theory of what a well-run PMO can do for a business, the functions it can perform and how it should sit in the governance of the business then they will feel much more comfortable giving their opinions, desires and concerns.

STRUCTURE, NOT STRAIGHT JACKET

The main aim for these interviews is to ensure everybody has had the chance to have their say; therefore following a loose structure where you make sure that the same major questions are asked is important. However, this is not like an audit where the structure can be so rigid that it limits proper conversation. It may also be an idea to conduct the interview with two people from the project team. This allows for the following advantages:

- It allows the PMO project manager to be there as the 'face' of the project while also calling on the services of a specialist business analyst.
- It allows the second person to ask relevant supplementary questions that the first person may not have thought of.
- It reduces the chances of certain topics not being covered or certain questions not being asked.
- It allows for post-interview 'debriefs' where agreement can be reached on how different comments from the interviewee should be interpreted. Different people can pick up on different nuances and points of emphasis, especially if the interviewee is trying to be politically sensitive in what they are saying.

The requirements gathering workshops should happen with key representatives of diverse groups of stakeholders, including, as previously stated, each organisational support function. Again, it may be necessary for an initial session to include a briefing on what are the main, potential functions and purposes of an effective PMO, together with setting clear expectations of what is required from the workshop and the method to be used to achieve this.

Again it is best to conduct separate workshops for different groups of stakeholders and to focus different workshops on the different layers of portfolio, programme and project management. Inevitably this will lead to working with different types of stakeholders anyway.

As different subjects are discussed, such as risk management, specific requirements will be captured and documented. Later these will be analysed in detail but for now it good to gauge some idea of their relative importance. A useful way of managing this is to quickly classify each requirement as it is captured using the MoSCoW system.

MoSCoW is a technique that was first developed at Oracle Corporation for software development. However, it has since been incorporated into the Business Analysis Body of Knowledge (A Guide to the Business Analysis Body of Knowledge (BABOK) is the written guide to the collection of business analysis knowledge published by the International Institute of Business Analysis (IIBA) and can be used on any set of requirements, such as these.

A further explanation of MoSCoW can be found below.

M – Must Have

Requirements classified as *MUST* are critical to project success and their inclusion in the scope is imperative. If any of these requirements are not implemented then it could be considered that the project has not met its scope objectives and is considered a failure. It is important to avoid the temptation to classify every requirement as a *MUST* straight away. In any case, these can be downgraded subject to agreement based on their relative importance to other requirements at the end of the exercise.

S – Should Have

SHOULD requirements are important to project success and would only not be implemented in the face of severe restrictions on time and budget. Alternatively, *SHOULD* requirements can be as important as *MUST*, although *SHOULD* requirements may not be as time-critical or may have workarounds, allowing other ways of satisfying the requirement.

C – Could Have

Requirements labelled as *COULD* are less critical and often seen as *nice to have*. It is often good to include some specifically for stakeholder engagement purposes, particularly if they are simple to implement. They may be important in the eyes of the stakeholder who raised them but less so in the overall picture of the project as a whole.

W – Would Like

These requirements are either the least-critical, lowest-payback items, or not considered appropriate at the time. These requirements, while still being important, may be implemented if there is extra budget or time available or if it makes sense at the time. Stakeholders should agree this and look for opportunities for their inclusion.

Tools

Following on from the work that was done in the previous stage to assess the tools situation, it would be a good idea in this stage to begin looking at tools requirements also. However, it's important that these will not be finalised in this stage. Tools should be driven by the business processes they enable, not the other way round. Therefore, generally final tools requirements will not be generated until after the Design stage. However, at this point some high-level requirements can be captured which will help to build up an overall picture of the final solution.

Output

The output of the Assemble phase will mostly be a set of requirements documentation; that is to say, a series of documents or a single report outlining the organisational requirements for the new PMO. These requirements will have already been prioritised and will be broken into the different levels (portfolio, programme and project) and into the various knowledge areas of each of those areas.

It is also imperative that the requirements documentation includes a traceability matrix. A requirements traceability matrix ensures that each and every requirement can be traced back to the requirement or the individual who raised it. Ideally there should also be a short rationale for having the requirement. This may seem superfluous at this stage but later in the project when the PMO is being implemented some requirements may appear baffling and it may be long forgotten how and when they were raised. Each requirement should also have a status and an owner.

In addition there should be an agreed process for managing requirements, including managing changes to the requirements and merging them with other requirements, etc. This should form part of the overall management plan governing the project as a whole.

At the end of the Assemble stage all stakeholders should be aware of the possibilities of this project and they should feel like they have been given their say in what the eventual outcome will look like. These workshops and interviews are a crucial part of the change management process and the requirements that come from them form the main input into the next stage where they will be analysed and consolidated to form the basis of the future PMO.

Analyse

The purpose of the Analyse stage is to take the data obtained from the Assess stage and the requirements obtained from the Assemble stage and to begin to fashion them into an understanding of what needs to be achieved to build the PMO that the organisation needs. The main output (see Figure 6) is a gap analysis of the gulf between the 'As-Is' and 'To-Be' states which will ultimately be presented to the Steering Committee for approval in the first major Go/No Go Presentation.

The first major task in this stage is to analyse the assessment data to spot any disparities between the requirements that have been gathered and the situation as assessed. For example, to solve a problem of over-allocated resources it may have been stated that a strong requirement was the need for a resource allocation system for project resources. This would provide better control, clearer visibility and remove the duplication of resource commitments that appear to be the problem.

However, the assessment could have revealed that the real problem may lie not in the visibility and accuracy of the project level resource allocation (they may have a perfectly adequate system already), but in the lack of capacity management or prioritisation at portfolio level – that is no consideration is given as new projects and programmes are sanctioned by the organisation (presumably to support the strategic intentions) and more and more is 'pushed in to the project sausage machine'. A planning assumption of infinite capacity capability which is never the reality.

Other things that may come to light are that opinions given in the requirements workshops and interviews may differ and conflict between individuals or departments. The example below shows an extract of the results of one module of an online assessment conducted in an early part of the Assess stage. This particular chart gauges the level of agreement between different groups of stakeholders of different perspectives on the organisation's project management capability. In some, such as 'Community of PM Practice exists' and 'Programme Management Framework applied' there is a high level of agreement between the stakeholders. However, in some areas such as 'Project prioritisation applied' and 'Key project reviews exist' the stakeholders are split right down the middle on their opinions.

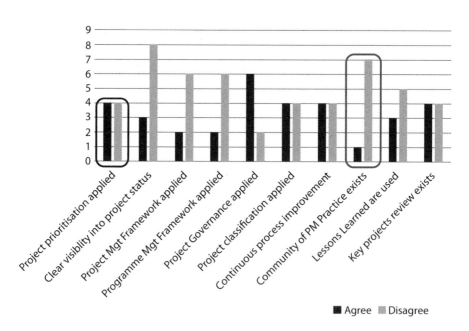

FIGURE 7.4 GAP ANALYSIS

Both areas need to be looked at and cross-checked with the outputs of the requirements workshops. It may be that one department or individual professes to have everything under control in one of these areas and has therefore not included it in their requirements. This may contradict the findings of the assessment and will need to be revisited. If a full maturity modelling exercise was carried out as part of the Assess stage, such as OPM3, it should be possible to check the records of the audit to see if the process has indeed been cited as in existence and in use. If it is found that there is a disparity between the assessment results and the requirements of the organisation then it may be that a new requirement needs to be created or an existing one may need to be reprioritised. This is an iterative exercise but such review and consolidation forms one of the focal points of the Analyse stage.

BEST-PRACTICE BENCHMARK

Another area of focus for the analyse stage is to compare both the assessment results and requirements aspirations against commonly accepted best practice.

A well designed assessment (such as the output of an OPM3 audit) should have done this for the organisation's processes anyway and you will need this sort of guidance to achieve this step. The alternative, assuming that you don't have such benchmarks to hand, would be to engage one of the Systems Integrators or industry specialist consultancies – the preferred and recommended option is to use a good tool.

An extract example of this type of output can be seen below in Table 7.2.

TABLE 7.2   ASSESSMENT OUTPUT EXAMPLE

ID	SOLUTION OBJECTIVE	GAP DESCRIPTION	BEST PRACTICE ID	BEST PRACTICE NAME	ADDITIONAL COMMENTS
				Programme Resources Process	
			1410	Manage Organisational Project Management Resource Pool	
15	Implement a resource control mechanism to enable the simple assignment, tracking and approval for project effort	Inadequate project monitoring and control arrangements	See additional comment		All Pre-Go activities to be treated as 'start up' phase which precedes Programme/ Project initiation

TABLE 7.2   CONTINUED

ID	SOLUTION OBJECTIVE	GAP DESCRIPTION	BEST PRACTICE ID	BEST PRACTICE NAME	ADDITIONAL COMMENTS
16	Evaluate current project management	Currently, there are inefficient and/ or inappropriate project management processes which are viewed as a hindrance rather than enablers to the PM community	2190	Benchmark Organisational Project Management Performance Against Industry Standards	
			3050	Perform Benchmarking to Improve Performance	
17	Quicken the recruitment search and approval process by removing some of approval signature requirements	Lengthy and tedious approval processes resulting in being unable to hire the right people	1590	Record Project Resource Assignments	
18	As part of the Tools Report, complete an analysis of ERP and key processes	Issues with current system(s)	7365	Project Management Information System	Proposed PMIS to offer all functionality currently offered by Oracle ERP
19	Implement a mechanism to promote the collaboration	No unified mechanism for collaborative assessment and selection of suppliers and/ or solutions	1210	Standardise Conduct Programme Procurements Process	
			3655	Standardise Conduct Programme Procurements Process	

This part is quite straightforward; processes can be compared very easily and written very easily. However, in our integrated approach we also need to adopt the principles of Assess, Assemble and Analyse for People and Tools.

For the People component there needs to be a similar process of benchmarking, though it is more difficult to ascertain where people 'should' be in terms of competency. Using the competency frameworks described in the Assess stage it may be possible to factor in where each individual should be based on their job title and years of experience. The idea is to try and benchmark each individual assessed based on their experience, job title and competency results against a competency development pathway based on training, coaching and mentoring.

The kind of disparities common to this kind of exercise include mismatches of job title (for instance, the individual may have the title programme manager or project director but are, in reality, performing a straightforward project management role and not displaying the characteristics or attributes of either of those more elevated roles.

By placing individuals on this scale as a result of the assessments conducted in the Assess stage we can benchmark each individual based on where they should be and develop a tailored competency development programme for them to get them there. In this way, we are conducting a similar gap analysis exercise to the process component but, together with the tools analysis which is ongoing in the background, we are doing it in an integrated way to ensure the best mix of initiatives occur in the right order and at the right speed to develop the organisation's P3M capability to the level they require.

Go/No Go meeting

Once the Assess, Assemble and Analyse stages are completed, the 'A' phase of the project, there should be a Go/No Go meeting scheduled with the Steering Committee, chaired by the Sponsor. This is effectively a controlling stage gate before moving on.

It's important in this meeting to cover the following points:

- Summary findings from the Assess stage:
    - brief explanation of assessment methodology;
    - strengths and weaknesses found;
    - breakdown of scores by business unit and/or geographical reasons;
    - performance implications: how these findings are impacting the business.

- Overview of main PMO requirements:
  - brief explanation of requirements methodology and which groups and individuals were involved;
  - summary of major requirements and deliverables;
  - performance implications: what benefits will this bring the organisation?
- Findings from the Analysis stage:
  - highlight perceived disparities, trends and observations from the analysis: what were the main surprises?
  - overview of the major gaps that need to filled in process, people competency and tool functionality.
- Overview of project performance (KPIs, schedule, risks, etc.).
- Briefing on the D phase:
  - What are the next steps? Who will be engaged? What can they expect to see?
- Presentation of the emerging Target Operating Model.
- Q&A/Discussion.
- Official acceptance of the A phase and authorisation to move forward to the D phase.

Notice that the main objective of the meeting is to leave with authorisation to proceed to the next phase. This means that each member of the Steering Committee will already be familiar with the ins and outs of the project. Some of them may have been interviewed as part of the Assess or Assemble stages, or they have delegated the role to a technical advisory committee who have met recently and grilled the project team already. Or individual members of the Steering Committee have already had private briefings to ensure their expectations and concerns have been addressed before the full committee meeting. These are the things that will ensure good project becomes a great project and one that proceeds through its phases unhindered. Essentially, if the right stakeholders have been engaged in the right way then the Go / No Go meeting should be a formality.

Target Operating Model

One of the elements presented in the Go/No Go meeting is an emerging Target Operating Model. The Target Operating Model is essentially a visualisation of how the PMO will look, how it will function and where it will sit in the business. It is almost a blueprint of what will be built and the finished version is the key output of the Design stage.

However, following the A phase the project team should have a good idea of how a proposed Target Operating Model will look. The purpose of including a first pass at it here is because it is a preview for the audience of what is to come; it is a prelude to the next stage and the next phase but, more importantly, if the purpose of the Go/No Go meeting is to engender support for the project at the highest level and obtain authorisation for the next phase then showing them the latest thinking on how the PMO is going to look is imperative.

Outputs from Phase 2

The following are the typical outputs from the second phase of this framework:

- Project Management Competency Assessment.
- Health Check Report.
- PM Tools Report.
- PM and Business Interface Environment Report.
- Maturity Assessment Report.
- Training Plan.
- High-Level Requirements.
- Gap Analysis.
- Future PM Organisation Detailed Report.
- Improvement Road Map.
- PMO Awareness Training.
- Project Catalogue.
- Go/No Go Presentation – Leading to the approval to proceed.

CHAPTER 8

Phase 3 – Set Up PMO (D Phase)

FIGURE 8.1   PHASE 3

If managed correctly the Go/No Go meeting now gives the project team a strong, renewed mandate to create and deliver the PMO. Where previous efforts in the A phase have focused around understanding the need for the PMO and the scale of the task involved, the D phase will focus on finalising the detail of how the PMO will look, what it will do, what needs to be done to build it and the steps needed to roll it out.

TABLE 8.1   SET UP PHASE (D PHASE)

OBJECTIVES	KEY ACTIVITIES	BENEFITS
• Establish the PMO in the various branches leveraging on phase 2	• Establish the PMO Governance Model • Develop the Organisation and Structural Functional Model • Develop project management methodology • EPM Solution and Design • EPM Proof of Concept • Develop transition strategy • Change management determine measurement of change	• PMO capabilities will be set up (scope, time, cost, quality, communication, risk, procurement, financial, stakeholder and governance)

Design

The phase starts with finalising the design of the PMO (see Table 8.1) and takes as its primary input the Target Operating Model that was accepted in principle in the Go/No Go meeting. If the Target Operating Model was a high-level view of how the PMO would look then in this phase we need to delve into the detail of that to determine the individual functions it will perform.

As we've discussed earlier in the book, no two PMOs are the same and a successful PMO has to reflect the needs of the organisation it is being built to serve. Of course this is very much on the agenda at the Assemble stage when gathering requirements but it is now at Design where the individual functions of the PMO need to be decided upon. This inevitably goes hand in hand with the level of authority that the PMO will have within the organisation and it is this point specifically that may be politically charged.

Imagine a classic matrix organisation where projects are delivered across different functions within a business and projects are being run in all parts of the organisation with different types of sponsors from different business units and functions. It may be fine for the PMO to perform a service where it supports these projects or provides advice to the project managers but how would the organisation react to a PMO that could intervene, deprioritise or even cancel that project if it didn't fit into the wider need of the portfolio?

TYPES OF PMOS

It is generally accepted that there are three broad types of PMO.

Supporting PMO

The supporting PMO is sometimes referred to as the 'Weather Station' model because its primary role is to view and report. It's involvement in the day-to-day business of projects is passive in that there is no direct management or intervention in the projects that they support. Moreover it may provide 'on-demand' project management expertise to those people that need it. It may be the custodian of a methodology and template library but it does not enforce it. It will usually, however, endeavour to collect as much information about project status as it can to be an 'information-hub' for the business. It may make recommendations to the business about actions to take but is not empowered to take any action itself. It may also provide administrative support for project managers where needed. As such, these types of PMO are sometimes referred to as Project Support Offices (PSO) to describe their function more precisely.

The limitation here is that organisations stay around level 1 of the project management maturity model because project managers are not required to comply with any central methodologies.

Controlling PMO

A Controlling PMO is sometimes referred to as the 'Control Tower' model, principally because, as well as the visibility of a Supportive PMO, it also has the remit to intervene where necessary to ensure smooth running of project activities. Controlling PMOs are usually empowered to achieve consistency of approach and performance across the portfolio of projects they support; as such they tend to exist to ensure that the organisation consistently achieves a maturity level of around level 2 in the project management maturity model. They achieve this by ensuring compliance to a best-practice method, perhaps by conducting regular project audits or reviews which could occur randomly or at predetermined points in the project life cycle, such as around phase gates. They are usually empowered to require that project managers follow a certain process or use certain templates and they may also take the role of intervening in under-performing projects, perhaps coming up with project recovery plans with corrective actions to get the project back on track.

The danger of the Controlling model is that the PMO is seen as a bureaucratic overhead whose only function is to impede project progress with box-ticking exercises. It can also create politically charged conflicts in matrix environments due to the shared authority in the project. It therefore needs the visible backing of senior management if it is to have any hope of achieving its goals.

Directive PMO

The Directive PMO takes the direct involvement in projects one step further by actually being the line management body commissioning and directing the projects themselves. In this model, the PMO owns and allocates the project managers to individual projects in the portfolio. This removes the conflicts of the Controlling PMO as the reporting line of the project is clear. It also makes it easy for the PMO to enforce common practices and standards. When managed well it can create a specialist pool of project managers whose competency set is known, managed, developed and used to inform proactive and intelligent resource allocation. Reporting methods and tools can easily be standardised and project prioritisation is more straightforward owing to the high degree of visibility and control of the portfolio.

While a Directive PMO is good for a predominantly 'projectised' environment, it is not necessarily the ideal model for every organisation. A common problem with Directive PMOs is gaining buy-in from the business for the projects it runs. For business change projects it requires project managers with high degrees of stakeholder management skills because the project sponsors may not necessarily feel 'ownership' of the projects themselves.

Blended PMO

There is another way that PMOs can operate and that is a combination; a mixture of directive, supporting and controlling, better described as a 'blended' approach. The blend may involve any two models or a combination of all three.

In many ways this view of the role of a PMO in the organisation is over-simplified.

Many PMOs show different characteristics depending on each individual project. It may, for example, predominantly perform a Controlling role but take a Directive role for key projects, especially ones that directly affect project management, such as the implementation of an enterprise project management system. Moreover, the role of the Supporting PMO could in itself be split into three major functions, the first one being the 'custodian of best practice' in the organisation, defining the methodology and templates to be used, the second providing administrative support to project managers, and the third to act as the 'information-hub', a one-stop-shop for information about project status.

Clearly the role of the PMO needs to be delineated into these more specific functions and the guidance issued from the Axelos (a new joint venture company, created by the Cabinet Office on behalf of Her Majesty's Government (HMG) in the United Kingdom and Capita plc to run the Best Management Practice portfolio) in the form of P3O (Portfolio, Programme, Project Office) states various different functions that a 'P3O' can perform. It groups these into three major areas as laid out on Table 8.2.

TABLE 8.2 P3O FUNCTIONS

P3O		
PLANNING	**DELIVERY**	**CENTRE OF EXCELLENCE**
Portfolio build, prioritisation, analysis and reporting	Monitor, review and reporting	Standards and methods (processes and tools)
Programme and project set up and closure	Risk, issue and change management	Internal consultancy
Stakeholder engagement and communications	Finance	Organisational learning and knowledge management
Planning and estimating	Commercial (including supplier management)	People and skills (P3M competencies)
Capacity planning and resource management	Quality assurance	
Benefits realisation management	Information management (incl. configuration and asset management)	
Performance monitoring	Transition management	
	Secretariat	

P3O discusses how these functions could be sliced up between different levels of PMO; for example the Centre of Excellence functions could be performed by a central 'Hub' Enterprise PMO while the Delivery functions could be performed by numerous 'Spoke' PMOs or PSOs in different departments, business units or regions. The Portfolio functions could then be performed by the separate BAU functions that are commissioning the projects. In another scenario where a single PMO is the hub of all project activity, all the functions could be performed in one place. In this scenario the PMO would require a wide range of competencies at its disposal, as we will see when we deal with the Deploy stage.

It goes without saying that these competencies are found in the specialisations of different individuals so the functions that the PMO will perform will heavily influence how it is staffed. Therefore the PMO organisation chart, for both where it fits into the organisation and what individuals it is made up of, becomes a key output of the design stage and the most tangible view of the Target Operating Model.

The first thing stakeholders will want to see is where the new PMO structure sits in the existing organisation and this will heavily depend on the functions that the PMO needs to perform. For instance, a Supportive PMO carrying out mostly Centre of Excellence duties can almost sit 'on the side lines' removed from the day-to-day bustle of the line management functions or the pool of project managers. If, however, the PMO is performing Portfolio-level functions, perhaps within a more Directive style, you would expect it to be front and centre on the organisational chart overseeing all change activity. In this case in particular, it works best if the PMO then has a direct input into the board or even a presence on it.

DESIGNS OF PMOS

As discussed above, P3O has some suggestions of how to divide up the various roles and functions that broadly fit into the following models.

Hub and Spoke

A 'Hub and Spoke' PMO design describes a system of organisational design for P3O where there is a centralised office (the hub) connected to a number of smaller decentralised offices (the spokes) each with a sub-set of the centralised office's business objectives, functions and services. All information and processes (connections) are arranged so that they move along spokes to the hub at the centre. A Hub and Spoke model provides the benefit of scalability for large organisations and supports business ownership by maintaining a level of decentralisation

The hub component is permanent and manages and oversees project or programme reporting, planning, quality assurance, standards enforcement and enhancements and manages a flexible resource pool.

This is often linked to some form of Portfolio office that offers strategy support, prioritisation guidance, benefits Management capability and Portfolio Dashboard(s).

Command Central

The Command Central approach is often associated with the Directive model as it benefits from that kind of direct control over the portfolio. However, these kinds of PMOs can still operate as Supporting or Controlling models without the more direct aspects like scrutiny and challenge. Some Portfolio and Delivery functions such as Benefits Realisation, Dashboard Reporting and Contract/Vendor Management can still be performed on a passive or 'on-demand basis.

PMO ROLES

PMO Lead

It is an interesting trend in the development of PMOs that, at this level of maturity, this PMO Manager or Director role is starting to overlap significantly with our understanding of the role of the Portfolio Manager.

By assuming direct control of the portfolio, this role now naturally falls to the PMO Manager whose key position is interpreting corporate strategy into the makeup of the portfolio. It is for this reason that this role is sometimes being called the PMO Director or could assume other such lofty titles such as Head of Change, VP of Projects or Portfolio Director.

The role remains the same; the corporate board needs enterprise oversight of the portfolio with a clear line of sight on status, progress, risk and spend. There needs to be clear accountability through a well maintained and enforced governance structure which enables shifts in the corporate strategy to ripple through the organisation in the shape of reprioritised objectives, adjusted scoping of projects and resource reallocation. This can only be achieved if the PMO has the visibility and control to make these decisions.

Other PMO Roles

The Centre of Excellence coach role could also be combined with the PMO Manager or the Methods & Practices role in a smaller organisation. The role focuses around being an 'internal consultant' to the organisation and providing the voice of experience to the PM community. Because of this the role is suited to somebody with many years' experience as a project manager; somebody who can empathise with project managers and guide them through difficult situations. Having developed in their own right through a project management career they can then also advise on career and competency development for project managers themselves. This plays a delicate balance against the 'thought leadership' role which requires a strong theoretical approach to P3M so that industry best practice can be built into the methods used in the PMO. Not all people can balance this 'real world' experience with the theoretical expertise and, as such, these roles may be performed by different people.

The Reporting Coordinator is somebody with strong organisational skills but also needs strong people skills. Their role may involve chasing project managers for the latest status reports or risk registers from their projects and it is important that this is done in such a way to avoid resentment from the PM community towards the PMO. Reports then need to be prepared in such a way that the crucial trend and decision-making information is clearly visible. In smaller PMOs this role could also provide Secretariat or administrative support to the PM community, such as taking and preparing minutes of project status meetings.

The Methods and Practice role is principally there to ensure compliance to the methods and tools used throughout the portfolio. They will ensure adherence to the chosen methodologies and may conduct project and programme audits and reviews for this purpose. In a large PMO the responsibility of administering the enterprise project management system would be a separate role and may require multiple personnel.

Equally the compliance function may be developed into a separate Quality Assurance role, but in smaller PMOs both would comfortably sit within this role. The Methods and Practice role may also be responsible, perhaps in tandem with the Centre of Excellence role, for the induction of new project and programme managers and ensuring that they have a competent working knowledge of the methodologies, tools and systems used at the organisation.

Depending again on the scope of the PMO, there may also be a specialist Business Analyst or Business Analysis team that forms part of the PMO and are responsible for the requirements gathering for new projects. This is a specialist function that can be deployed for each project for a limited time and, as such, may legitimately form part of the services offered by the PMO. In a similar vein, as shown in the diagram, a Directive style PMO would also then be directly responsible for a team of project and programme managers also.

This is by no means an exhaustive list of roles needed. As discussed above, there may be a need for specialist teams in charge of quality, risk or administration of the enterprise project management system. In addition, depending on the type of business, the PMO may need its own support functions like IT, HR or legal, as well as specialist contract or commercial managers, facilities managers, trainers and even marketeers (as we shall see in Deploy). In short, its scope could stretch to being a sizeable business unit of any organisation.

Therefore the scope and role of the PMO is a crucial thing to agree with the business as early as possible. At this stage we are looking to crystallise this in the PMO charter.

PMO CHARTER

The Project Management Body of Knowledge[1] tells us that every project should begin with a project charter. It is the document that sets out the business need or the opportunity. It demonstrates why the project exists and why it is viable and justified. Most importantly, it appoints and empowers the project manager to begin managing the project on the sponsor's behalf; it is a document of authorisation.

Similarly, we think of chartered accountants or surveyors, being authorised by their governing body to go about their work but they are chartered for specific things, so the scope of their work is clear. When a public body refers to their charter they mean the mission that they have been entrusted with; the set of activities they should be doing and the outcomes they have been constituted to achieve.

In this sense a PMO charter is no different. It is the defining document of the PMO because it explains why it exists and for what purpose, what it aims to achieve and what is the scope of its remit. In many ways it is the definitive outcome of the Design stage because it embodies the very essence of what the PMO is about, and this may take several rounds of discussion and conjecture to agree upon, depending on the political nature of the organisation. It is in this document that the roles and functions we have discussed are crystallised, signed off and formally accepted by the business. Indeed, more than acceptance, the desired nature of a charter is such that the PMO is now mandated to carry out these functions and achieve these outcomes with all the authority permitted by the governance systems in the charter. It is now on a mission and without this document, it would be rudderless. Typical contents or heading of a PMO charter would include:

- Overview and Objectives:
    - Background/History.
    - PMO Vision, Mission and Values.
    - PMO Goals and Objectives.
    - PMO Success Criteria and Performance Metrics.
    - Benefits of the PMO.
- PMO Scope:
    - Organisational Context and Interaction with Existing Departments.
    - PMO Governance Structure and Authorisation Levels.

---

1   *A Guide to the Project Management Body of Knowledge* (PMBOK Guide) is a book which presents a set of standard terminology and guidelines for project management. The 5th edition (2013) is the document resulting from work overseen by the Project Management Institute (PMI).

- PMO Organisation Chart.
- PMO Roles and Responsibilities.
- PMO Functions and Services.

Once the PMO charter is agreed upon, signed and distributed the PMO is now a formally chartered body of the organisation and should begin meeting with the frequency and purpose specified in the governance section of the document. Hereafter the project board for the project to implement the PMO may now report to or may directly merge with this new PMO structure, as the first thing they will be doing is overseeing the creation of the systems, processes and tools needed for it to fulfil its mission.

Develop

Now that the PMO is formally chartered and the scope of its responsibilities and functions are clear, the detail of each of these functions needs to be defined and built as per the requirements defined in the Assemble stage. It is important to note that the Develop stage does not have to be complete in order for the Deploy stage to begin; indeed, there is more than likely to be significant overlap between the two. For example, if the organisation has chartered the PMO to achieve level 3 maturity in the first two years across the areas of project, programme and portfolio management, for example, that is a lot of change for an organisation of any size to absorb, depending of course from where they started.

With this in mind, new processes and guidance will have to be rolled out as a staggered approach and so development work will initially focus on those areas that need to implemented first to ensure early benefit for the organisation. It is here that a PMO Roadmap is needed, which will determine the levels of maturity the PMO can expect to demonstrate at what time in what function. From this, a full schedule of work can be created by the project team but first the roadmap must be agreed. Roadmaps come in all different shapes and sizes but on the following pages is an example of a simple approach incorporating the idea of achieving ascending levels of maturity in each PMO function over time.

The PMO Roadmap contains various functional areas and maps the PMO's expected development by maturity stages against a five year timeline. The maturity stages are mapped from 1 to 5 in rough accordance with the levels described in the project management maturity models earlier in the book. Maturity Stage 1 is the lowest level, and stage 5 is the highest. The following table explains the five maturity stages.

TABLE 8.3   PMO MATURITY

MATURITY STAGE	GENERAL LABEL	GENERAL DESCRIPTION
1	Ad hoc	No common approach. Performance is not repeatable.
2	Standardised	Common approach defined. Performance is not repeatable
3	Managed	Approach is adhered to. Performance is repeatable.
4	Controlled	Performance is consistent, predictable and objectively measured.
5	Optimised	There is an ongoing culture of Continuous Process Improvement.

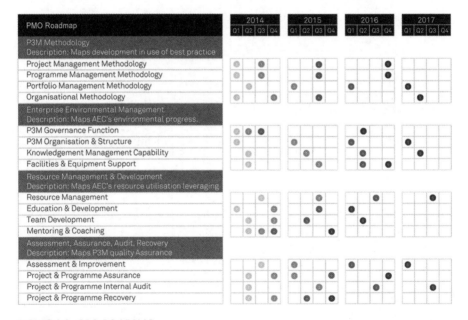

FIGURE 8.2 CPO ROADMAP

Table 8.4 explains the functional area maturity descriptions for the PMO Roadmap.

TABLE 8.4 FUNCTIONAL AREA MATURITY

FUNCTIONAL AREA	MATURITY STAGE 1	MATURITY STAGE 2	MATURITY STAGE 3	MATURITY STAGE 4	MATURITY STAGE 5
1. PROJECT MANAGEMENT METHODOLOGY	Employs Standard life cycle processes and Tools when available or ad hoc	Introduces critical processes, practices and tools of project management	Establishes and monitors use of a complete project management methodology	Enhances content and monitors used of a comprehensive PM methodology	Assesses methodology and perform continuous process improvement
2. PROGRAMME MANAGEMENT METHODOLOGY	Employs standard life cycle processes and tools when available or ad hoc	Introduces critical processes, practices and tools of program management	Establishes and monitors use of a complete PgM management methodology	Enhances content and monitors used of a comprehensive PgM methodology	Assesses methodology and perform continuous process improvement
3. PORTFOLIO MANAGEMENT METHODOLOGY	Employs processes and Tools when available or ad hoc	Introduces critical processes, practices and tools of portfolio management	Establishes and monitors use of a complete portfolio management methodology	Enhances content and monitors used of a comprehensive PPM methodology	Assesses methodology and perform continuous process improvement
4. ORGANISATIONAL CHANGE MANAGEMENT	Little or no change management applied and People dependent without any formal practices or plans	Some elements of change management are being applied in isolated projects. But many different tactics are used inconsistently	Comprehensive approach for managing change is being applied in multiple projects and examples of best practices are evident	Organisation-wide standards and methods are broadly deployed for managing and leading change and common approach has been selected	CM competency is evident in all levels of the organisation and is part of the organisation's intellectual property and Continuous process improvement in place

TABLE 8.4 CONTINUED

FUNCTIONAL AREA	MATURITY STAGE 1	MATURITY STAGE 2	MATURITY STAGE 3	MATURITY STAGE 4	MATURITY STAGE 5
5. P3M GOVERNANCE FUNCTION	The concept of project governance does not formally exist; however, the authority is conveyed by a project charter	Introduces essential Governance processes and tools but no formal training or communication on governance standards and responsibilities	A baseline set of governance has been defined, documented, implemented and tracked	Governance has evolved into an enterprise-wide process and activities are becoming integrated with the enterprise governance process	Governance Processes have been refined to a level of external best practice, as a result of continuous improvement
6. P3M ORGANISATIONAL STRUCTURE	Standard Project Team member roles and Project stakeholder not defined	Establish essential project roles and relationships (internal business units)	Introduce and evaluate a project management and PMO Structure	Expand project management and business alignment (Bus Strategy –> CPO –>PMO)	Review and Analyse Project and Programme organisation and structure effectiveness
7. KNOWLEDGE MANAGEMENT CAPABILITY	Use standard knowledge management tools when available (planning, reports) or ad hoc	Introduces essential project information capability (reporting procedures and tools)	Introduces automated tools and practices for project knowledge management	Expands knowledge management tool functionality for business use (PPM tool)	Analyses PKM system capability and recommends advanced project KM tools
8. FACILITIES and EQUIPMENT SUPPORT	Use facilities and equipment needed to accomplish the project effort when available	Ensures reasonable facilities and basic equipment are available for the Project or Programme	Identify F&E requirements, Monitors F&E assignments and manage F&F disposition	Expand support capability to include facility acquisition	Conducts/ performs project and Programme facility and equipment optimised use and cost analysis

TABLE 8.4 CONTINUED

FUNCTIONAL AREA	MATURITY STAGE 1	MATURITY STAGE 2	MATURITY STAGE 3	MATURITY STAGE 4	MATURITY STAGE 5
9. RESOURCE MANAGEMENT	Ad hoc project resources acquisition and assignment coordination	Prepares essential project resource utilisation guidance	Implements complete project resource management guidance	Manage Project Resource Standards and Performance	Collaborates with HR and Business Units to determine resource utilisation
10. EDUCATION and DEVELOPMENT	Coordinates project team member participation in required training and assists project team members to plan career progress activities	Identify needs, facilitates training course participation and introduces Project Management as a Professional discipline	Establishes, manage a formal training curriculum and manage s project management career development programme	Extends project management environment training to other stakeholders and provide project management career planning and counselling assistance	Uses Training results in strategic business initiatives (credentials in marketing)and monitors Business interest fulfilment and value from career development
11. TEAM DEVELOPMENT	Manages individual integration into project teams	Introduces concepts of project team dynamics	Establishes, manages and incorporates practices into pm methodology	Extends Practices to develop project manager leadership skill and capability	Conducts research and analysis of team performance
12. MENTORING and COACHING	Not applicable at this stage	Introduces project management mentoring on an as-needed, as hoc basis	Establishes a formal project management mentoring programme	Policies and Guidance for mentor programmes is developed	Mentor Programme evaluation and examination is accomplished

TABLE 8.4 CONTINUED

FUNCTIONAL AREA	MATURITY STAGE 1	MATURITY STAGE 2	MATURITY STAGE 3	MATURITY STAGE 4	MATURITY STAGE 5
13. ASSESSMENT and IMPROVEMENT	Participates in PM competency evaluation when available	Conduct essential evaluations (PM Skill, PM Processes, etc. ...)	Conduct complete assessment (Competency, Capability, Tools and PM maturity	Conduct Advanced assessments (Governance, Enterprise-level capability)	Consistent frequency of Reassessment in the enterprise and extend the assessment to external stakeholders
14. PROJECT and PROGRAMME INTERNAL AUDIT	Ad hoc project health-check and review	Establish basic project health-check	Establish Project Auditing Capability across all projects	Expands Auditing efficiency through training (provide PM self-audit training)	Conducts Project Audit Analysis to improve auditing effectiveness
15. PROJECT and PROGRAMME ASSURANCE	Ad hoc project and programme assurance	Create Preliminary Guidance for Project/ Programme Assurance	Develops Capability to conduct Project and programme Assurance activities	Introduce project/ Programme Assurance Management and tracking tools	Conduct Project /Programme Assurance Analysis towards achieving goals of continuous improvement
16. PROJECT and PROGRAMME RECOVERY	Ad hoc Project Control	Create Preliminary Guidance for project control	Develops Capability to conduct project and programme recovery activities	Introduce project Recovery Management and tracking tools	Conduct Project Recovery Analysis towards achieving goals of continuous improvement

TABLE 8.4 CONTINUED

FUNCTIONAL AREA	MATURITY STAGE 1	MATURITY STAGE 2	MATURITY STAGE 3	MATURITY STAGE 4	MATURITY STAGE 5
17. CORPORATE PORTFOLIO OFFICE	Provides data to high-level oversight authority for consolidation when request	Introduce the fundamental concepts of Project Portfolio Management	Develops Policies and guidance to support effective PPM	Establishes and manages collaborative processes for PPM	Create Comprehensive Project Portfolio Management Capability
18. BUSINESS PERFORMANCE MANAGEMENT	Not applicable at this stage	Facilitates Business Practice Integration	Coordinates and deploys project management based business solutions	Serve as Project Management and Business Advisor to SEM	Analyse Project Performance for Business Results

Once a PMO Roadmap has been agreed then the task begins of creating the various processes needed to get the organisation to where it needs to be. The principle reference, as well as the Roadmap itself will be the requirements documentation and gap analysis performed in the A phase.

Work should now start on documenting all the processes needed to achieve a level 2 maturity across the board. The business analysts involved in the A phase should have some involvement here but the main skills employed by the project team will be technical writing, as a large part of the initial work will be to write a definitive reference manual for how the PMO will go about managing the projects, programmes and portfolios under its charge.

Major artefacts to be produced in these frameworks (see Table 8.4) will include the following.

PMO MANUAL

This will be a detailed description of how the PMO conducts its business, building on the PMO charter. A good way to structure it is go function by function and discuss the processes and tools required to perform that function, as well as making clear who is responsible for it. A major part of this will be the project management methodology.

METHODOLOGIES

Project Management Methodology

The project management methodology is the collective approach to how projects are managed and, as such, is key to how the PMO commissions and oversees the projects it supports. The methodology should have a common project life cycle with predetermined phase gates and a clear view of what activities are to be performed in each phase and which documents should be prepared.

PRINCE2 (PRojects IN Controlled Environments) is a widely used project management method that navigates you through all the essentials for running a successful project. It is an example of a robust and complete project management methodology as it brings basic controls such as approval gates and change control procedures to the project environment. The objective of the PMO is to ensure each project reports its status in the same way, in a common life cycle and with a common terminology so that it is possible to compare the progress and performance one project versus another. Having this common, documented approach is the main factor in moving from a level 1 maturity to a level 2.

Programme Management Methodology

Like projects, programmes are also finite and should have a predetermined life cycle. Unlike projects, however, they are fluid and though the vision of what the programme is going to achieve is clear, what is less clear are the complete steps in how it is going to get there. Because programmes are benefit led, benefit profiling and mapping are pivotal to the programme management methodology and there should be clear connections in governance from the project layer to the programme layer.

Programme management is therefore both the process of managing several related projects, often with the intention of improving an organisation's performance, and the process of governing the overall 'programme' and defining, managing, and realising business benefits from the summation of the project activity.

Portfolio Management Framework

Note that at portfolio level the terminology changes to framework rather than methodology. Portfolios are permanent in their nature rather than finite and are constantly shifting in response to the organisational strategy. They sit astride multiple programme and project life cycles and, as such, function more as a framework of processes, tools and guidance rather than an end-to-end methodology.

Project Portfolio Management (sometimes referred to as PPM) is a management process designed to help an organisation to register and view information about all of its projects and programmes. With such visibility this allows such organisations to sort and prioritise each project according to certain criteria, such as:

- Strategic value.
- Cost.
- Impact on resources.
- Tactical need.

A PPM driven organisation will have, typically, a portfolio/project dashboard representing the overall health and status of each project as well as a formalised process for project updates, project reporting and escalation of issues.

In addition the portfolio connection to the sponsoring organisations strategy should be maintained.

TEMPLATE LIBRARY

Templates are generally much maligned and undervalued as a resource for the PMO and the project/programme manager. Their purpose is to structure people's thoughts and prompt the users to consider certain things in the planning process rather than skip over them or deal with them tacitly. One of the reasons that the perception of methodologies, and PMOs that govern them, are considered too restrictive is the inclusion of poorly designed templates.

Well written templates should be intuitive and easy to use, including only the information necessary to serve their purpose. The design should be simple, sharp and pleasant with a font that is easy to read; first and foremost, it should be remembered that these are communication tools, built to crystallise agreed decisions or intended paths forward. For the first-time user, they should come with guidance of how the template is used, why it is used, who is responsible for it and where it fits in with the overall governance structure. Each section heading should then include deletable prompts which explain what is trying to be achieved in each section. Too often, people just pay lip service to headings in templates, copying and pasting from other documents and not thinking about why the heading is there and what questions need to be asked to address it.

Typical templates that a PMO may need to put together include (not complete or exclusive):

Project Level
- Business Case.
- Project Proposal.
- Project Charter.
- Scope of Work.
- Project Initiation Document.
- Project Management Plan.
- Risk Register.
- Communications Plan.

- Work Breakdown Structure.
- Schedule.
- Roles and Responsibilities.
- Task Assignment.
- Change Register.
- Change Request.
- Minutes and Action Items.
- Issues Log.
- Project Kick Off Presentation.
- Project Progress Report.
- Post Implementation Review.

Programme
- Programme Brief.
- Programme Blueprint.
- Benefits Management Plan:
  - Benefit Profile.
  - Benefit Realisation Plan.
  - Benefit Review.
  - Benefit Sustainment Plan.
- Stakeholder Management Plan.
- Programme Roadmap.

Portfolio
- Complexity Assessment Criteria and Tool.
- Prioritisation Criteria and Tool.
- Portfolio Register.
- Portfolio Dashboard.

At the end of the Develop stage, the PMO should be equipped with a full range of documents and processes at each of the three management layers.

Deploy

As previously explained the Deploy stage can commence as soon as the first deliverables from Develop are complete and signed off. The idea in a phased approach to deployment is not just to ensure that the organisation doesn't have to absorb inordinate amounts of change at once but also that certain capabilities are prioritised with a view to providing some quick early wins for the PMO and to demonstrate as much value to the business as early as possible.

This may involve taking more of a hands-on approach in the short-term, like performing some project recovery services on projects that are clearly failing. It may be as simple as ensuring that all projects that need to be are closed so that billing can occur or resources can be freed up for other work. In a typical project environment, projects can continue due to dwindling, unresolved issues or lack of a joined-up administrative closure process so these are some practical areas where the PMO staff can have a quick impact.

It's important to note that the process of deployment has its roots back in the A phase. The process of assessing and gathering requirements should be treated by the project team as an opportunity to engage the various stakeholders involved and ensure that their needs and requirements are reflected back in the processes and tools that have been developed, hence the need for the requirements traceability matrix. A new way of working cannot just be inflicted on the user or the beneficiary environment without this prior engagement process and then the ongoing support that our model provides.

Change Management

Fans of change management may note that the PAD3T™ model we are describing is fully compatible with John Kotter's 8-step model to the Leadership of Change.

Dr John Paul Kotter (born 1947) is an author and American professor. He is currently the Head of Research at Kotter International and teaches in the High Potentials Leadership Program at the Harvard Business School.

His international bestseller *Leading Change* (1996) is considered by many to be the seminal work in the field of change management. The book outlines a practical 8-step process for change management:

1. *Establish a Sense of Urgency*
    By objectively assessing the current status and, as much as possible demonstrating the business impact and opportunity cost of not having proper governance in place, the organisation as a whole gains a recognition that the change needs to happen.
2. *Create a Guiding Coalition*
    Earlier in this book we were at pains to emphasise the role of the Sponsor and the project board. It is crucial that senior representatives

of the major areas affected are part of this body and are actively engaged. It is this group of people that is the main factor on whether the PMO will have the authority levels that it needs to ensure that the change is successful.

3. *Create a Vision for the Change*

    The project sponsor should have articulated this in the charter so the vehicles are there. However, the main tool for gaining buy-in at the end of the A phase was the high-level Target Operating Model. This model, defined in more detail in the Design stage, is the vision of the transformed organisation and one that is tangible enough for everyone involved in the project to be able to understand and buy into as long as the benefits are continually reinforced and ultimately demonstrated by the project team.

4. *Communicate the Change*

    At a senior level this would be done in the run up to and at the Go/ No Go meetings at the end of the A and D phases. Kotter discusses how successful change requires at least 75 per cent backing from the organisation though and so on a broader basis the changes and the reasons and benefits thereof would be communicated through the marketing activities and roadshows dealt with in this chapter.

5. *Remove Obstacles*

    Obstacles to a PMO implementation are legion and complex. They can range from general indifference or misaligned expectations among the PM community through to outright hostility. They can be a limited circle of influence to make a real difference (for example not being able to engage the business or its support functions as part of the process) or just an inability or unreadiness to understand or adapt to the change in general. Proper planning and communication, constant monitoring of the project environment and strong sponsorship to remove these roadblocks will conspire to mitigate these factors.

6. *Create Short-Term Wins*

    As explained earlier in this chapter, it is crucial that the PMO begins to demonstrate value to the business as soon as possible. The PMO will be implementing guidance, processes and tools to manage benefits in a way that demonstrates measurable value back to the business. Just as it would seem remiss not to manage the PMO project as a model project, the benefits it brings should be managed and demonstrated in a similar vein. This serves the twin purpose of justifying the PMOs existence to any doubters that remain while also continuing to reinforce buy-in for the methods being used.

7.   *Build on the Change*

This is all about momentum and continuous improvement. Reward and recognition systems should be implemented for good examples of the behaviours being encouraged; champions and super users should be identified and used as advocates for the new approach, ideally by demonstrating that it works in the 'real world'. Organisation-wide lessons learned sessions should begin as soon as possible so that the PMO can learn quickly what is working and what is being adopted and what is not. On the results of that the PMO should be ready and prepared to change certain things if necessary and not to hold onto superfluous ideas if they are not working. This is embodied in the Enhance stage of the PADET cycle.

8.   *Anchor the Change into the Culture*

The Embed stage is all about this element, not just how to educate people on the new methods but how to ensure that the benefits being realised are sustainable. Individual targets and remuneration systems should be adjusted to reflect the new requirements and discussions at the top of the organisation should reinforce the key themes being encouraged by the PMO. New staff being brought on board should reflect these same attitudes and come ready made with the associated skills to hit the ground running in a professional environment. Finally, success stories and case studies should be drawn up and widely circulated – the perception of the PMO will be positive if it displays a positive image based on sound achievements.

Marketing Plan

Following on from Kotter's 8-stage process it is clear that it is not enough to create good output. For new capabilities to be accepted by the organisation it is necessary to create and reinforce positive perceptions of the change. Like any marketing campaign this involves considering the needs and expectations of the audience and thinking about how those needs can be met. It's about coming up with communication methods that cut through the noise of their perceptions and day-to-day activities to ensure the key messages are received and understood. Finally, marketing is ultimately about customer satisfaction so it makes sense to plan the deployment of the PMO like a marketing campaign.

Why is it that when we are in a new town and we are looking for some lunch or a coffee we tend to gravitate towards a brand we may already have in our own town? Branding is everywhere, in the clothes we wear, in the food we eat, in the consumer items that we buy. Brands can be about status or about how we define ourselves. They are not always about bland uniformity but they are always about confidence and reassurance. A brand sets expectations; it gives its customers the confidence of high performance and the reassurance that the performance will be consistent. Therefore it is a good idea to brand the PMO or the methods that it uses, after all, consistent performance is precisely one of the goals we are aiming to achieve.

Once the brand is established all sorts of associated marketing activities can be commissioned to reinforce and promote it. Templates and websites can carry the brand, as can stationery that can be issued to project managers. An exhibition stand can be commissioned and used to run a series of road shows. Other ideas for activities in the marketing plan can include:

NEWSLETTERS OR BLOGS

These are an excellent way to establish the PMO's thought leadership credentials while also raising awareness of its activities and services.

LUNCH AND LEARN SESSIONS

Not only a good way of making the PMO's activities visible and demonstrating the benefit of them being there. This is also a good technique to use in the Enhance stage to target specific improvements and deficiencies.

PRESS RELEASES

These are a good way of gaining visible top management commitment for the PMO and focusing on the benefits that it brings. By communicating the existence of the PMO externally as a positive news story that demonstrates it as part of the organisation's overall commitment to excellence, it helps the PM community to have pride and confidence in their work and how it helps the organisation as a whole.

AWARDS

An annual award campaign focusing around project or project team of the year can help to create a healthy sense of competition without individuals 'hogging' the limelight; which can, ironically, act as a demotivating factor in the project community.

SPONSORSHIP OPPORTUNITIES

Sponsorship or hosting of the local project group chapter events or similar can again help to reinforce the organisation's commitment to good P3M and also a good opportunity to keep senior management engaged in the subject. If the PMO is encouraging that project managers maintain a credential similar to the PMP (Project Management Professional) then these events can also assist in this process by helping credential holders with their continuing professional requirements.

All of these activities and anything else of their like are part of being able to raise awareness and create confidence that the new approach to project management is both credible and durable; that's to say that it will work in practice and will therefore not be just another management idea that turns out to be a flash in the pan.

Training

A process will not work if people do not know about it, hence the marketing plan. However, it will also not work if people do not know how, why or when they should use it. When performed and timed correctly training is an effective way of deploying these kinds of processes. Training sessions should look to integrate process, theory and practice. That is to say, if you are trying to deploy a risk management process then first ensure that everybody is educated on basic risk management theory: What is risk? Where does it come from? Why does it need to be managed? How does it behave across a project life cycle? What are some of the ways this is dealt with in organisations?

This should then be followed up with education on the way the process works: How is risk managed here? What are the standard categories of risks that we usually experience on our projects? How do we rate and prioritise risks? How do we quantify risk? What does our risk register look like?

Finally there should be some kind of opportunity to put this theory and process into practice via some form of case study or role play. In this way the cycle is complete; training attendees know what risk is and what the benefits of managing it are, they know which processes and tools that the PMO want them to use and they know how to use them in a realistic context.

Deploying Portfolio Management

Assuming that the PMO we are implementing has a charter to perform the full scope of PMO services, we need to consider how and when to implement our portfolio management framework. There is almost a case of the chicken and the egg conundrum here. In order for portfolio management to be effective it needs to have robust, consistent information being generated by its constituent projects and programmes, which would suggest that these methodologies should be fully deployed and in place before a framework is attempted at the portfolio layer. However, there are clear benefits to at least defining the portfolio early in the Deploy stage. Broadly, the major steps to implementing portfolio management are:

1. Obtain a single, complete view of the organisation's portfolio. This is predominantly an information gathering exercise and may have been carried out already in the A phase. The aim is to have a full portfolio register that includes any activity or 'component' that fulfils the criteria of project or programme. For each component it can help to put together a one-page Programme/Project Brief that should include purpose and objectives, costs, benefits, timeline, major risks and performance to date (if known).

2. This process can bring about significant and almost instantaneous dividends by removing any duplicate or unaligned initiatives. If the PMO charter has empowered the PMO to have control over starting, steering and stopping projects according to the needs of the organisation, then, by examining the organisation's strategy, components that are not directly contributing to it can be dismantled at will, saving unnecessary spend and resource consumption. Indeed,

this is one of the biggest business cases for portfolio management in general and one of the main reasons portfolio management initiatives have relatively rapid payback periods. Most organisations are involved in multiple streams of activity that do not directly contribute to its aims.

3.   Complete a portfolio delivery plan and monitor progress against it. Assuming that all components remaining are aligned with the objectives of the organisation the next step would be to organise them into a coherent delivery plan. Rather than checking for alignment and desirability the focus now shifts to achievability. A high-level delivery plan will be drawn up. Based on the complexity of the work streams, the required deadlines and the resources available; if it seems unachievable or too risky then some lower priority initiatives could be postponed or even cancelled. Meanwhile, implementing regular progress reporting will highlight gaps and stimulate further questions and debate.

4.   Start tracking completed versus anticipated component performance and use this to revise forecasts.

5.   This will improved business case discipline and accuracy of forecasting which will inevitably lead to improved investment appraisal and more informed portfolio prioritisation; by implementing rigorous evaluation clear messages will be sent that the advent of the PMO means a more rigorous and evidence-based approach to managing change.

6.   Review the portfolio and identify dependencies. This requires a more thorough review of the portfolio to not only identify where one initiative is dependent on the output of another, but also where several initiatives are competing for limited resource. This brings clearer visibility across the portfolio and, through proactive action, earlier resolution of potential problems before they occur.

7.   Establish clear governance structures. Here is where the portfolio management work can dove tail with the bulk of the work to implement the methodologies at project and programme level. The documentation of roles, responsibilities, standardised reporting and the subsequent training that implements it provides the base for effective governance at the portfolio layer and helps ensure decision-makers get the information they require to achieve their goals.

8.   Define a standard set of investment and appraisal criteria. Once the contents of the portfolio have been established and the rules that

govern them embedded it's necessary to put up some walls to prevent the unnecessary commencement of new initiatives that could reapply pressure on the capacity for delivery.

9.   Apply staged release of funding linked to stage/phase gates. Investment of resources is linked to confidence in successful delivery; rigorous start gates ensure that programmes and projects are initiated in a controlled manner

Outputs from Phase 3

The following are the typical outputs from the third phase of this framework:

- PMO Charter.
- PMO Road Map.
- PMO Execution Plan.
- PMO Marketing Plan.
- PMO Organisation Chart.
- PMO Manual.
- PM Methodology or Framework.
- Solution and Design Document.
- Stakeholder Map and Plan.
- PM Methodology Training and Deployment Plan.
- Organisation Change Plan.
- Communication Plan.
- Training Course(s) and Materials.
- Trainers.
- Go/No Go Presentation – Leading to the approval to proceed.

CHAPTER 9

Phase 4 – Operate PMO (E Phase)

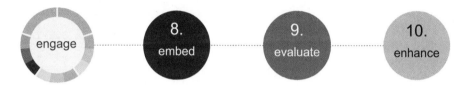

FIGURE 9.1 PHASE 4

Most PMO implementations finish at the Deploy stage and handover into an operational mode. The job is seen as done when documentation is complete and everybody is trained. This is where the E phase makes the difference between an average PMO and a successful PMO implementation. By embedding the new processes and behaviours you are ensuring that they become an ingrained part of the business culture and by evaluating and enhancing you are demonstrating measurable success and then making it even better. If this life cycle is planned from the start you will have a head start in delivering a successful PMO and the main difference will be found in these next few stages (Table 9.1).

TABLE 9.1   OPERATE PMO (E PHASE)

OBJECTIVES	KEY ACTIVITIES	BENEFITS
• Transitioning to delivery by executing the programme strategy plan, conducting methodology training, activating user feedback, mechanism and providing mentoring	• Conduct methodology user required training • Establish a PMO helpline or helpdesk • Facilitate executive management support • Promote methodology usage • Collate user feedback	• Provides centralised control of all objects under the PMO • Increases communications and coordination across all projects • Manages and controls scope, cost, risk and quality across all projects

TABLE 9.1   CONTINUED

OBJECTIVES	KEY ACTIVITIES	BENEFITS
	• Mentoring and coaching • Conduct methodology performance evaluations • Evaluate PMO effectiveness	• One place to go for all project status and communication • Reduced project costs • Increased resource utilisation across the organisation and matches skills to project needs • Teams are fully trained • Create prerequisites to handover PMO

Embed

When implementing new processes, methods or tools one of the key criteria for success or failure is adoption. The project management community may have a shiny new way of working but the question is always 'will people use it?' And will they use it in the way that it was designed to be used? This is the only way to ultimately realise the benefits that the organisation hopes for and it's also the reason why this stage is crucial to the success of the PMO.

It is not enough to conduct the deployment activities described in the previous chapter. In order to truly embed the PMO into the psyche of the organisation we need to look at ways to sustain the new methods and behaviours we have implemented. This is chiefly done through continuing the marketing activities described in the marketing plan we previously discussed as well as looking at identifying champions of the new method and combining that with intelligent use of teaming, coaching and mentoring. This must then be backed up and built on for the future by ensuring that new recruitment policies and personal development criteria reflect the competencies required from the business.

EXECUTIVE SUPPORT

Possibly the single most important factor to sustain the credibility of the new PMO is maintaining the visible support of senior management. Earlier we argued that to be a truly effective and mature PMO the sponsorship and ownership must come from board level. This must be clearly visible across the organisation and backed up by deeds. For example, when the PMO requires that a high-profile project be delayed or closed because it doesn't meet alignment criteria to the organisational strategy, this must be supported by senior management as this level of decision-making has been delegated to the PMO. More commonly, if the PMO is delaying the progress of a project because it hasn't met phase-gate criteria or is not complying with the agreed reporting requirements, any such decisions must equally be backed up by senior management.

Key to this also is that senior management take their P3M governance roles seriously. It is likely that they will be sponsoring or be sitting on the steering committees of key programmes and projects in the portfolio and if they are not performing these roles then it severely dents the PMOs ability to enforce these crucial governance roles throughout the organisation. To help ensure this happens, full commitment must be gained from senior management as and when the methodologies and governance systems are being designed in the D phase. It is important not to overburden the role of sponsor or it simply will not be fulfilled. So to ensure that sponsors and committee members must be actively engaged in the programme or project they are leading a delicate balance should be struck between formal steering committee meetings, formal reporting formats and frequency thereof, and unofficial updates from the programme or project manager. Management by exception as described in the PRINCE2 method is a useful concept to build into this culture.

PMO HELP DESK

When any new piece of software is implemented, after initial training there is a period of 'floor walking' for hands on support to deal with problems as they arise and thereafter there is usually some kind of continued support service in the shape of a help desk to deal with ongoing incidents and problems experienced with the system.

The same approach can be used for the new PMO and can be used as a key focal point of this stage of the marketing campaign. This service is an especially obvious component when a new enterprise project management tool has formed part of the PMO implementation but it could also handle day-to-day queries such as helping a project manager fill out correctly rate or score a risk or simply pointing out where the current version of the risk register is located. The point of this is that the PM community know that there is somewhere to turn beyond the training they have received. It is a practical service offered by the PMO which, to them, may be the most useful role it has and the role that brings the most tangible and obvious benefit to them. As we previously mentioned, to be successful, PMOs need to demonstrate real and perceived value to both the business and the communities they serve.

TEAMING, COACHING AND MENTORING

Earlier in this book we discussed at length the importance of an integrated approach to delivering your PMO, that is to not only consider the processes and tools that you are looking at but also the needs, competencies, expectations and motivations of your people. Therefore it stands to reason that when trying to embed new practices, these elements should factor highly in your approach.

Teaming is one of the single most effective ways to develop competencies in your people if it is planned correctly using the right information. From the A phase, you will have a full skills inventory of each of your project staff, from project coordinators and administrators right through to senior project and programme directors. This should be used by your new PMO to proactively resource appropriate resources to each component project or programme. The main factor to consider when allocating resources is whether their skill set and experience match the needs of the project. Another is whether they will be a cultural fit for the team working on the project. You do not want an entire team of visionaries without any completer/finishers to get the work done, for example. Another factor to consider is the long-term development of your project management community by strategically teaming certain individuals together in the hope that one may learn from the other. This especially works if, during the assessment process, you found that you have coordinators with the ambition and potential to develop into project managers. If they have been found to be weak on commercial awareness, for example, place them onto a project where they will be supporting a project manager who is among the best performing in this field. Not only will their competencies often naturally complement each other but the learning/mentoring process will be a source of motivation and satisfaction for both parties. In a world where good project management talent is scarce, a policy of 'growing your own' using techniques like this will deliver major savings on recruitment costs and rework in the long term.

COACHING AND MENTORING

Coaching and mentoring should be designed and built into the service catalogue of your PMO from the start and should form a key part of the Centre of Excellence functions. When we discussed the concept of competence in the A phase, we saw that competence isn't just made up of the knowledge you have acquired but also how you apply it. Training can give you the knowledge and the skills but coaching and mentoring over a period of time will develop competencies. Therefore, when considering the staffing of your PMO it is wise to employ experienced project managers in the field to act as mentors for the project manager community, helping them to apply the new theory they have learned and the new tools and processes that they have. In this way mentoring is formalised as a service that is open to all, whereas teaming can remain a more informal arrangement among the participants.

Coaching, however, should always be formalised, differing from the other two in that the coach does not necessarily need to be a subject matter expert in the industry or technical discipline of the person being coached. Moreover, they do not even need to be an expert in project management. Coaching is about working with the individual to set targets and goals that will improve their performance in the identified prioritised areas (that can also be found in the assessment results). It is about maintaining focus and momentum in the right path and again would benefit both the business and the individual and result in the PMO adding value to both.

RECRUITMENT AND PERFORMANCE MANAGEMENT

Another way to embed the values and priorities of the PMO into the organisation is to work closely with the human resources department on how project staff are recruited and managed. Change is difficult in any organisation and sometimes, depending on the level of resistance and/or ability among the team, one of the most effective approaches over the medium to long-term is attrition. This is relatively easy to achieve is most of the team is contract-based but this would often rule out the alternative of competency development anyway. Contractors should, in theory, come ready-equipped with the competencies needed by the organisation but the reality is often quite different, which is why it is often a good idea to include contract staff as well as permanent staff in your competency assessments.

Recruitment activity should come from an analysis of the competencies found within the organisation versus the competencies required, and this information should be found in the gap analysis conducted as part of the Analysis stage. Briefs given to recruitment agencies or departments should be competency focused and assessment centres should be designed and configured to yield objective scoring on them. It is important to include this step because the skill must be observed in action and tested in specific conditions to be a true competency. If the competencies required are not available in the current team they must be developed or brought in.

The same is true for management of project manager performance. In order to embed certain behaviours they must be encouraged or incentivised to display them and this should be done as part of the annual appraisal process. It is one thing to offer training, coaching and mentoring programmes as part of the PMO's 'soft power' but sometimes only true and complete change can be achieved when this is combined and complemented with more traditional approaches such as rewarding desired behaviour and penalising otherwise.

PERFORMANCE MANAGEMENT

A word here on the performance management of the overall project team (i.e. the resources used to perform project tasks). In a classic matrix organisation these resources are often owned by functional teams designed to carry out specific operational roles and they are drafted into project work on an 'as-needed' basis. One of the main challenges for project managers in these environments is ensuring that these resources complete the project tasks assigned to them when their priority lies with their operational work. In such cases where the contribution to the project is significant the project manager should have a partial input into the performance appraisal of the individual, thereby potentially affecting his or her bonus and/or advancement. In the case of programme management, senior functional managers identified as key beneficiaries of the programme should have clear accountability for the realisation and sustainment of the appropriate programme benefits. This, of course, requires the backing of senior management, as do most of the initiatives discussed in this section.

A CHAMPION IDEA

When deploying and embedding your new process or practice, in the face of resistance, scepticism and hostility, there is no substitute for clearly demonstrating that it works. In the A phase, it will have become apparent that some members of the community are more actively interested and supportive of the initiative than others. If this enthusiasm is matched by ability it is a good idea to 'recruit' them as champions of the new initiative. Champions should also be individuals that have earned the respect of their colleagues. Not only will they have played an active part in determining the needs of the community as part of the Assemble and Design stages but they will now help to embed the new practice by leading from the front. Their mission is to lead the use of the new methodologies and/or tools and chalk up some early success stories that can then be marketed throughout the organisation. This is largely an informal role but the right candidates will happily accept. It serves as a proactive way for the PMO to engage the project management community in an organic way rather than relying solely on didactic dogma and is also a way of demonstrating early success to the business.

One of the key aspects identified in the my book *Leading Successful PMOs* was that a good and balanced PMO will spent some of the time promoting and marketing and 'selling' the value of the PMO and the supporting methods and developmental services, as well as articulating the great job that the project managers were doing for the business.

Take every opportunity that you can to market, promote and sell the value of the PMO. In time you may choose to develop a PMO services menu (what the PMO does and how to request such a service) but in the early days offer your help wherever there is an opportunity. A proactive approach helps open doors to the PMO and it will start people talking in a positive way about the PMO work ethic and capability. This can be done through any way you think is appropriate:

- Newsletters (PM community ones and company ones).
- Showcases (presentations, lunch time sessions, case studies, etc.).
- Intranet presence.
- Post-project reviews (PMO attendance and write ups).
- Project manager of the year awards.
- Project of the year awards.
- Marketing 'goodies' with the PMO 'brand'.
- Project manager peer recommendations (about the PMO value).

- Executive declarations.
- Offering 'project management for non-project managers' training outside the PMO/project community.
- Blogs.
- Podcasts.
    ... and much more.

A little marketing and self-promotion goes a long, long way (don't be shy!).

Evaluate

After deployment, embedding activities will begin and somewhere around these initiatives there will be a 'Day 0' where the PMO will be officially launched. As with any project this will be an authorised milestone, probably at the phase-gate between the D and the E phases. Unlike a traditional, sequential life cycle, however, the Evaluation activities will begin from this point and will therefore probably run parallel with much of the Embed activity. The idea being that, as the PMO is embedded into the organisation, the results of the Evaluate stage will demonstrate a constant improvement.

To that regard this stage has a dual purpose. The first is to fulfil the undeniable need to demonstrate that the PMO is improving the performance of the business. The second is to identify what initiatives are working and which ones are not, as to expect that all new initiatives will be runaway successes would be a naivety. The output of these evaluations will then feed into the analysis and resulting improvements of the Enhance stage.

In order to measure success or otherwise it is necessary to have a benchmark. The importance of this was discussed back in the A phase and there are various steps to ensure that the process adds value. The first must come directly from the PMO charter. Looking at the purpose of the PMO and what it hopes to achieve we can work out what outcomes need to be measured and what performance indicators need to be monitored.

PERFORMANCE INDICATORS

There exists a veritable plethora of performance indicators and ratios that can be monitored. The important thing is to ensure that they indicate whether key outcomes are being achieved without overcomplicating the process or creating a culture of targets or quotas. Some of the main indicators that can be used are listed below:

- Percentage of 'successful' projects. (What success looks like will need to be defined for example it could be the classic 'OTOBOS' (On Time, On Budget, On Scope) or other factors could be considered, such as customer satisfaction scores).
- Average project length and cost.
- Ratio of permanent staff to contract staff in project teams.
- Percentage of projects achieving 'green' compliance ratings from audits.
- Average number of projects managed per project manager.
- Correlation of successful/failed projects versus any other variable.
- Overall amount of schedule slippage at any one time.
- Number of missed milestones in a given time period.
- Average and overall amount of schedule and cost variance in the portfolio at any one time.
- Ratio of project management effort to overall project effort.
- Average number of days that any issues remain open.
- Benefit Cost Ratio (BCR) – looks at the overall difference of each project's costs versus its benefits. A BCR of 1.2 is, relatively, a more 'profitable' project than one with a BCR of 1.1.
- Average resource utilisation.
- Average work package total effort.
- Distribution of 'high' and 'low' risk projects in the portfolio.
- Average number of changes in the project life cycle.

AUDIT

The word audit tends to be accompanied by visions of cheerless old men scrutinising binders full of mind-numbing documentation, but when used wisely a well-run audit programme can be one of the principal sources of continuous improvement activity. The trick here is not to have audits perceived as trying to 'catch out' uncompliant project managers but as a means of understanding what is working and what is not working in the organisation. If a certain template is not being used, then rather than just recording it in the audit, the auditor should endeavour to find out why. Is it because the project managers didn't know the template existed? Is it because they didn't know how to use it? Is it because they didn't have time to do it? Or perhaps it's because they just don't see the value in it. All of these root causes need to be captured because they tell a different story and warrant a different response when we think about enhancing our PMO.

This is one advantage of having the auditing of the project and programme environment conducted by the PMO rather than an organisation's existing internal audit capability, which may only be concerned with pure compliance. Auditing can occur at any point in a project's life cycle but it is often recommended to coincide with stage or phase boundaries for the following reasons:

- Helps with early identification of problems.
- Instils consistency and rigor at stage boundaries.
- Clarifies performance/cost/schedule relationships.
- Improves project performance within its life cycle (rather than at the end when it's too late).
- Identifies future opportunities.
- Evaluates the performance of the project team.
- The resulting report confirms the project status with its stakeholders.
- Reconfirms feasibility, viability and commitment to project.

HEALTH CHECK

A health check is different to an audit in that it does not check compliance against a standard. In a project or programme health check we are looking more at performance and risk. For example, how is the project performing against its objectives? Is the project under control? Is there an acceptable level of risk? Does the project status reflect the true picture? Crucially, what are the perceptions of the stakeholders?

In this last point a 360-degree survey similar to the 'P3M-Pulse' used in the A phase may be a good regular tool to 'check the pulse' of individual projects across the portfolio. If projects are scoring well in audits but are scoring low in health checks, it's likely that the documentation is being done but that it isn't serving its purpose, or at the very least, the perception of project performance is low among the business stakeholders – this is something the PMO needs to know in order to target improvements.

There are many different frameworks that can be used for project health checks but as a general rule, any project health check should at least cover elements of the following 10 points:

1. Strategic Alignment: Is it clear where the project contributes to your strategy (do you need to review this) and is the priority well understood and communicated?

2. Business Case: Is the project justified on a strong business case, is it still current, are business requirements still appropriate, are agreed critical success factors clear, and is there significant user involvement?

3. Accountability: Is clear ownership for the project outcome established? Is there an experienced project manager accountable for execution? Is an active senior sponsor ensuring organisational challenges are dealt with? Is there a clear structure ensuring all parties understand their accountability?

4. Active Governance: Is active governance in place that not only establishes corporate controls but also harnesses management support, steers the project, removes obstacles and remediates project or benefit-realisation shortfalls? Are support structures in place for defining problems and solution options for clear and swift decision-making?

5. Planning: Has a useful plan been agreed with the necessary stakeholders? Is it broken down into manageable pieces allowing the organisation to commit to one stage at a time? Is it realistic in relation to current organisational constraints (people/time/budget/feasibility)? Does it align with the business case and current requirements? Have the key risks that may impact the success of the project been identified?

6. Control: Is the project being executed in manageable stages with periodic reviews and progress updates? Is there a simple and effective method of escalating problems? Is effective change, issues and risk management in place to safeguard your investment? Have the key risks that may impact the success of the project been mitigated? Are you looking to reduce complexity at every opportunity?

7. Impact and Benefits: Are plans in place for how the organisation will accommodate transition changes that the project will introduce and how benefits will be embedded and measured? Is any significant organisational resistance being managed with the executive team?

8. Resourcing: Are the right people on the project or just the available people? Are there adequate resources allocated and does the organisation understand the importance of their prioritisation and commitments? Are internal and external resource performance monitored proactively?

9.   Communication: Are key stakeholders kept informed? Do you trust the information being reported, and is it effective? Does communication identify risks, clearly defined problems and resolutions agreed rather than share information? Does communication promote realistic expectations? Is adequate notice provided? Are communications events planned or a reaction to complaints?

10.   Executive View: Is there a high-level map of all major initiatives, how they benefit the organisation and impact each other? Are major initiatives reviewed when the strategy changes? Are the organisation's project and programme skills evolving into a mature core capability?

PORTFOLIO REVIEWS

Audits and health checks are two complementary components of an overall quality management system to be owned and administered by the PMO as part of the overall governance model. However, regular project and programme status reports should still be providing consistent feeds of data which can enable the PMO evaluation criteria to be tracked and monitored. The principal vehicle for looking at the progressive performance against these criteria would be the portfolio review.

At a portfolio review the portfolio manager will present the status of both the main individual components (programmes, projects, etc.) and the overall portfolio itself. This will include many of the performance indicators already discussed in this chapter.

Enhance

Any project management maturity model acknowledges that there is no such thing as perfection. The highest accolade an organisation can achieve, usually a level 5, is a recognition and assertion that its people, processes and use of tools and technology are geared towards a culture of continuous improvement. Once processes have been designed, built and embedded into the organisation through careful change management the challenge is then to optimise them to constantly strive for 'ever improving results'.

Imagine the lap times and pit stops of a Formula 1 team. At the highest level, there will not be great variation in terms of seconds between the average times achieved. However, there is a constant search and culture of experimentation to try modifying specific variables and empirically measuring the effect this has on the performance times. For example, in the 2012 season the Red Bull team introduced a new feature on their car called a diffuser that increased downforce, making the car 'stickier' on the road and able to take corners slightly faster. This improved lap time performance by only a fraction but it was enough to have a significant effect on races. Until it was observed and mimicked by competitive teams, Red Bull enjoyed a considerable competitive advantage but this was only achieved through a continuous and painstaking culture of measurement, experimentation, testing and modification. Dave Brailsford achieved unprecedented success with the British cycling team and called it the culture of 'marginal increments'. Anything can be measured and enhanced in the same way, using basic quality management techniques. Using the metrics from the Evaluate stage which are regularly gathered through things like timesheet reporting, surveys and status reports, performance can be tracked over time and analysed for trends and opportunities for improvement.

STATISTICAL PROCESS CONTROL

Let's say one of the metrics being monitored in a portfolio of software development projects was how many coding errors found per sprint or iteration,

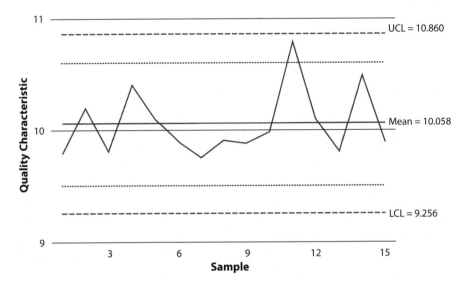

FIGURE 9.2 STATISTICAL PROCESS CONTROL

and that the average number was 5. With 5 as the mean, this metric would be monitored across each iteration within each project in the portfolio and tracked on a control chart, similar to the one in Figure 9.2 on the previous page.

With 5 as the expected mean, the PMO might decide that the maximum tolerable errors in any sprint is 10 (the Upper Control Limit, shown above) and any more than that would warrant an investigation, the process being 'out of control'.

Statistically, if 5 is the mean then results of regular metrics should hover mostly around the 4, 5 or 6 mark with some exceptional outliers. One scenario is, that as the metrics are taken it becomes noticeable that the average number of errors rises to 6 because scores start moving to a more common range of 5, 6 and 7. Although these scores still fall within the PMO's tolerable quality level of 10 errors per iteration, it is evident something has changed to cause a slightly higher error rate and this must, in turn, also be investigated. Typically, this happens when there have been 7 scores on one side of the mean (so instead of scores with a pattern resembling something like 4, 6, 4, 5, 8, 4, 3, 3, 5 it moves to something like 4, 5, 4, 6, 6, 7, 6, 8, 6, 7). As a general rule, after 7 occurrences of scores falling on one side of the mean there must be an assignable cause and this would also warrant further investigation. The objective here would be to find out what has changed in the process to cause a variation in the outcome. By understanding which factors directly impact the performance of our project work we can gradually start to identify clear ways of enhancing our performance.

FISHBONE DIAGRAMS

When we identify that something is significantly influencing our performance, for better or for worse, it is then a good idea to identify exactly what that variable is. A simple tool to use is a Fishbone or Ishikawa diagram – see Figure 9.3.

On the right is the effect, in this case an unacceptable number of coding errors per sprint across the portfolio. On the left are all the potential causes of this. The idea is to deliberate with those involved and find the root cause of the problem (or indeed, unexpected improvement).

When a cause it is assigned it is logged and then used for future trend analysis. A crucial step here is to group the causes correctly, and in a way that will be useful for us to determine the most significant influencing factors on the performance of our projects.

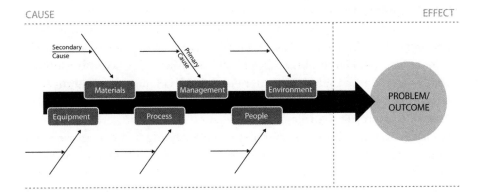

FIGURE 9.3 ISHIKAWA OR FISHBONE DIAGRAM

PARETO ANALYSIS

If the assignable causes are logged using consistent categories, then over a given time period it will begin to become apparent that certain factors are causing more problems than others. Let's say, for example, that a wine company wants to analyse where the majority of its problems come from. Each time a problem is reported they will use tools like the fishbone diagram to determine the root cause and log it over time. In the example below the various causes of complaints or returned or rejected wine are listed, together with the number of times they occurred.

In this case, the main causes of problems could be traced to inappropriate storage of the wine, both by the transporter and the consumer. This falls in line with Pareto's general point that 80 per cent of your problems are caused by 20 per cent of problem types. We could apply the same technique to analysing the occurrence of different types of coding errors in a software development portfolio or the causes of installation delays in a telecommunications network.

In general, the result will be the same and by knowing where the majority of our issues are we can target and optimise our improvement initiatives. Our wine producer, for example, might launch a project to educate the consumer about proper storage techniques or select a more specialist transporter. In the next time periods the causes of common problems may then be different but the cycle of continuous improvement carries on.

LESSONS LEARNED

This would hopefully strike the average project professional as a relatively obvious place to find improvements but it is surprising to see how often lessons learned are not used to their full potential in PMOs. Some organisations have managed to establish a culture of ensuring lessons learned are populated via a template or project management information system. However, few places then have a defined and integrated method of analysing that information and practically feeding that back into the project environment, so the process is ultimately bears no fruit.

It is well known and often emphasised in many project management methodologies that lessons learned should be a defined part of every project life cycle. It is often associated as a project closure exercise, when in fact it should be more associated as a phase closure exercise at the very least. In fact it should be a continuous process thought about and revisited almost as frequently as the risk and issue registers. By leaving lessons learned sessions until the end of the project, we are effectively not seeking the opportunities to benefit from them in that actual project. If we conduct lessons learned exercises throughout the life cycle, we can adjust the performance of each individual project.

Above and beyond individual projects, however, one other main objective of lessons learned is to share this learning with the rest of the organisation so that other project managers may benefit. Ideally it should be an integral source of intelligence for the Enhance stage and also a core part of the ongoing continuous improvement strategy. Below are some suggestions to help achieve this:

- *Do it for them*: Obviously the project managers themselves are in the best position to conduct lessons learned sessions but they may be in a political environment that makes it difficult or they may be unable or unwilling to find the time. In these cases the PMO can add lessons learned sessions to its 'service catalogue' of support it provides to the community. If the PMO conducts these sessions with the project manager and project team, the observations are more objective, but also the PMO obtains a greater visibility of the portfolio and therefore a deeper understanding of the issues at hand than it would from mere status reports.
- *Make lessons learned available*: One way to do this is to ensure lessons learned are accessible on a central project management information system. This is a 'pull' style communication and could therefore either

be in a specific folder on the system or promoted on the Wiki page of the PMO. Taking this one step further, the ideal approach would be to analyse lessons learned from around the portfolio and consolidate the recommendations into a searchable knowledge base. Knowledge management is a key driver of continuous improvement and ensures that as and when project managers encounter a problem they are able to actively search for pre-categorised solutions and recommendations.

- *Feed back the output*: Where a knowledge management system would provide a place for project managers to actively search in their own time, the PMO also needs to find ways to feed back the output of lessons learned sessions in a more 'push' style of communication that will reach project managers in a practical way. This could include having lessons learned as the basis of articles in the PMO's newsletter or the subject of talks at any internal conferences or gatherings. One practical way is for project managers to take it in turns to present lessons learned from their current project at a given time each week or month. This could be a scheduled section at team meetings or away days or more informal gatherings, perhaps accompanied with food and drinks over a lunchtime or on a Friday afternoon.

In each case, one of the primary objectives is to demonstrate value back to the project management community so that these systems and sessions contain practical advice based on real scenarios that can make their lives easier. The other is to ensure that the PMO learns more about the nature of the portfolio and combines this data with that gathered from reports, audits, health checks, reviews and other project and programme touch points so that they can be subject to Pareto Analysis and turned into targeted improvement initiatives.

Outputs from Phase 4

The following are the typical outputs from the fourth phase of this framework:

- PM Help Desk.
- Review and Feedback Process.
- Training Sessions.
- Mentoring and Coaching Sessions.
- PM Methodology or Framework Effectiveness Survey.
- PMO Assessment Report.

- PM Process Guide (update).
- PM Practice Guide (update).
- PM Template Library (update).
- PMO Manual (update).
- Go/No Go Presentation – Leading to the approval to proceed.

CHAPTER 10

Phase 5 – Transfer PMO

FIGURE 10.1 PHASE 5

In an established PMO the cycle we have discussed, from Assess in the A phase to Enhance in the E phase would continue to roll on. Assessment would occur on a regular basis, perhaps annually, and serve as a way of objectively measuring progress and improvement across the portfolio. As strengths are consolidated and new weaknesses are found, the cycle will play out again until new initiatives are complete and their output embedded, evaluated and enhanced. If, however, the project is to implement a PMO then at some point the time will come to hand over the reins to operations, as would be the case with many of the projects being supported by the PMO. In these cases, where a project manager has been allocated to set the PMO up and then hand it over, or if the PMO has been set up by consultants, a Transition phase is necessary (Table 10.1), to ensure a structured handover to the business.

TABLE 10.1 TRANSFER PMO

OBJECTIVES	KEY ACTIVITIES	BENEFITS
• Shut down the programme, release and transition the support of the PMO to the appropriate organisation staff, and preserve relevant data and knowledge gained during the course of the programme	• Develop programme closure report • Submit all artefacts to PMO • Assure that all the deliverables established in the programme scope have been completed • Acquire final lessons learned • Close financial and engagements contract • Release programme resources	• Operational PMO • Complete PMO handover • Ongoing visibility and control of project portfolio

Transfer

Like any project, the transition should be planned in advance and the main objective is for it to be as smooth as possible. In the PMO charter, ownership and staffing of the PMO should be clear, so the blueprint is mapped out very early in the process.

If new staff are required to run the PMO then it could be worth hiring them well before the end of the implementation cycle, perhaps even in the Embed stage but certainly at some point during the Evaluate stage. This gives them a chance to be involved with the day-to-day running of the PMO before they assume accountability for it. It also gives them the chance to feed and observations or suggestions they have into the improvements suggested and undertaken during the Enhance stage. This, in turn, allows the eventual PMO staff to have their input into how the PMO operates and therefore minimises the risk of blaming any problems they face on the processes they inherited (a natural human tendency when under pressure).

The types of activity required for a smooth transition include:

- Documentation, documentation, documentation. This is far from glamorous, but there is no other way to ensure a common reference point for people working on projects and in the PMO. In every workplace there are usually several individuals who know how things should be done, whom to speak to and where to go to get the right tools for the job. This tacit knowledge is crucial to the day-to-day running of the business and these people often thrive upon their usefulness and ability to help others. This, however, is no comfort when they are either too busy, have fallen ill or have moved on from the organisation. The only way to ensure that this knowledge remains is to translate it to the printed page.
- It is the message of consistency again. How does McDonald's ensure that a Big Mac tastes the same whether you go to Birmingham, Bogota or Beijing? They do it by regulating and documenting the process that produces it so it can be taught and referred to by hundreds of thousands of staff worldwide.
- Policies, processes and procedures do not have to take up volumes and volumes of folders; they should be clear and easy to refer to, catering for different learning styles. For example, there should be a visual depiction of the process, often using swim lane diagrams, as well as a concise narrative description walking the reader through what needs

to be done and by whom. A swim lane diagram is a type of flowchart, and it can be used to display the same type of information. What makes a swim lane diagram unique is that the flowchart objects are kept in lanes grouping them together. These lanes help visualise stages, employees, departments, or any other set of separated categories. The majority of this work should have been done in the Develop stage but a final check should be done here before any handover of PMO activity.

- Showing the ropes. If the time affords it then the incoming team should spend time with the incumbents. Job-shadowing is a very effective way of facilitating a smooth handover and ensures full knowledge transfer beyond just a quick series of handover meetings. Again, if this happens during the E phase the incoming team can observe the governance in action, gain feedback from and interact with the project management community and form their own judgements on what it is working and what could be improved in the Enhance stage.

Outputs from Phase 5

The following are the typical outputs from the fifth and final phase of this framework:

- Lessons Learned Final Report.
- Project Closure Report.
- Close (Go/No Go) Presentation – Leading conclusion of project.
- Maturity Re-Assessment.

End of the Journey?

And so you have your new PMO, planned, designed, embedded inside your organisation and now transferred to the resources that will lead it and tacit forward in to the future. The work is completed and the job is done.

Well certainly the life cycle framework we recommend and have followed in the preceding chapter, known as PAD3T™ (Figure 10.2), is completed but that is not the end of the road.

All being well then, the PMO will move forward from strength to strength but it is critical to not consider a PMO as a 'fixed beast', set up in one way that

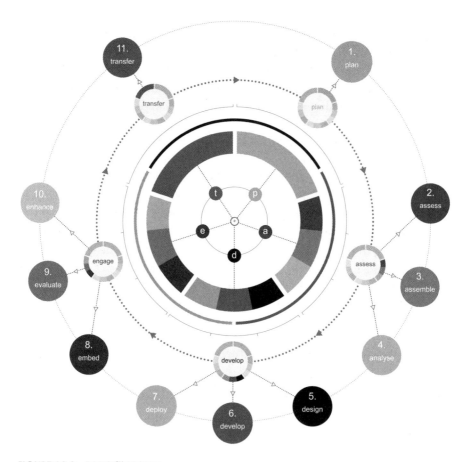

FIGURE 10.2   PAD3T™ MODEL

this will suffice for the foreseeable, and perhaps not foreseeable, future. IN fact one of the key natures of a PMO is that is the very opposite, it needs to be relevant to the business or organisation it serves and it needs to stay relevant, and this more than likely require it to evolve and change over time.

It is, of course, also possible on the other hand that maybe things aren't going quite as well as you had hoped or had planned for?

In either case you need to take regular action and take the 'pulse' of the PMO to make corrections or improvements as required.

Typically you will need to return to the business case. Here are some questions that you might ask of yourself and of the PMO:

- Has anything significantly changed in the business that requires an adjustment by the PMO?
- What is the view, within the business, of the value of the PMO?
- Are there any key opponents to the PMO operation?
- Are the methods you have established well adopted and adhered to, and have recommended improvements been acted upon?
- Has the level of project maturity risen?
- Are project managers reporting the same issues as before?
- Has there been a change in the PMO sponsorship role(s), personnel or approach?
- Has project 'health' improved or stagnated?
- Is the PMO approach the right one?
- Is the PMO model the right one?

You may need to survey the PMO stakeholders to understand in more detail what it is that needs extra effort and focus. Alternatively it may be that you just need to get together with your PMO team and revisit the PMO purpose.

Considering the maturity of PMOs then the aspiration will be to 'move up the levels' and at level 5 (see Table 10.2) we can see that the focus is very much on 'Continual Improvement' and 'Innovative Changes' both of which require a high level of self-evaluation.

TABLE 10.2 PMO MATURITY

1	LEVEL 1 – AD HOC	• Few formal definitions • PMO is a trouble shooter
2	LEVEL 2 – STANDARDISED	• Project disciplines in place – repeatable behaviour • Standards and Method and simple measures
3	LEVEL 3 – MANAGED	• Aligned with business goals • PMO is governing, reporting and correcting
4	LEVEL 4 – CONTROLLED	• Quantitative goals set • PMO KPIs in place
5	LEVEL 5 – OPTIMISED	• Continual improvement • PMO drives innovative changes

The Best PMOs

What can we say about the best PMOs out there? How do they behave, what do they do, how do they support the project community, the project based activity, and the organisation they belong to?

- The best PMOs have consistent, repeatable Project Management practices across the enterprise. All projects are held to the same standards and requirements for success. They have also eliminated redundant, bureaucratic Project Management practices that have slowed down projects.
- The best PMOs have the most experienced Project Managers in place and have a programme underway to recruit the best Project Managers, develop their existing Project Managers into the best and to maintain this level of quality and experience.
- The best PMOs have clear visibility into the progress and cost of all projects. They also know exactly how resources are being used. They openly share this information with all the appropriate stakeholders throughout the enterprise.
- The best PMOs adapt to the enterprise's strategic expectations and know how to operate effectively within the corporate structure and culture. And they are not rigid in their own structure and focus in order to adapt and adopt quickly.
- The best PMOs sponsor training and facilitate communities of practice to promote PM best practices in their organisations. Such communities of practice provide PMs with a forum to share their knowledge and share experiences.
- The best PMOs are the custodians of a dynamic framework of method to assist PMs in the delivery of projects. This includes not only process but also templates and guidance.
- The best PMOs ensure that quality assurance actually delivers quality.

Make your PMO the best it can be.

> **"**Life is a succession of lessons which must be lived to be understood. **"**

> Helen Keller

CHAPTER 11

Lessons Learned

The authors have certainly 'lived' the experience (and in fact more than one experience) of developing and deploying a significant PMO and from these experience comes the framework for a PMO life cycle as previously explained.

Also from this comes a number of 'lessons learned' that you should consider in your own PMO development.

Lesson One: Get Help

As has been already discussed the reality out there in 'PMO land' is that there is not a plethora of wise and experienced PMO managers, directors, leaders, heads, etc., and so it is sensible for anyone who is engaged to help an organisation set up a new PMO or advise on improvements to an existing PMO to reach out for some help.

The risk to not doing so is to, at the very least, slow the return on investment of the new PMO down. With a practical framework for guidance, such as this book, and a supporting experience coach then the organisation benefits that have led to the PMO investment will be secured in an optimum time frame and with reduced risk of failure.

This book is aimed as one source of aid, inspiration and guidance, so 'well done' for starting the process with the right attitude.

In addition this is what the authors, and others, do for a living so professional consultancy is another way to improve your chances of success with that PMO project.

And there are communities you can connect to – on LinkedIn, through the project management bodies such as PMI and APM, etc.

Do your research before jumping on too deeply.

Lesson Two: Get the Right Leader

Having the right 'head' of the PMO is also critical, in *Leading Successful PMOs* the top five attributes for a great PMO leader were explored:

> *The good PMO leaders must champion project management and project managers across their organisation as well as believing in the business strategy. They must communicate with conviction and negotiate fairly but strongly for the PMO and the projects. They must be enthusiastic about leading change and critically must have the strength of belief in their own uniqueness and that of the PMO they lead.*

It addition it is noted in the *PM-Partners: PMO Trends 2012* report:

> *When a PMO is expected to work across the organisation at all levels, oversee significant investments and facilitate senior decisions – it is surprising that a high number of organisations either put the wrong person in the job or don't support them when they are in place.*

Getting the right leader of the PMO is linked to lesson number one – you, and your organisation, will want to minimise the risk to PMO failure and maximise the time to ROI. As such having the right person leading that PMO is critical to its success – it is unlike any other managerial role in many ways.

Lesson Three: Measure the PMO Value

A 'balanced' approach to a PMO was advocated in *Leading Successful PMOs* with one way to achieve such a balance was to consider structuring your efforts under the '5 Ps':

- P = People.
- P = Process.
- P = Promotion.
- P = Performance.
- P = Project Management Information System.

The point here being that it may be tempting just to think of the PMO as all about the process, the means to ensure that good project management is achieved through methodology and quality assurance etc. but that ignores the people side.

And it may be that your consideration is towards the project management community and your focus is drawn towards the people (projects are all about people after all) and so you direct your efforts as a PMO leader towards training and team building, etc., but this ignores the project mechanics.

You may also accept the need to build a good tracking and reporting system, supported by an investment in a project management information system, to deliver the visibility of project health and progress towards business goals.

But without the inclusion of a promotional programme it could well be the case that all of the good work you, and your team, achieve in the areas of process and people will go unnoticed and unappreciated by both your peers and the executive.

It is our belief that the best PMOs balance all of this to achieve the most effective development of capability, representation of capability and sharing of capability and achievement.

In the PWC Insights and Trends: Current Portfolio, Programme, and Project Management Practices report there are a series of Key Findings and one relates to measuring value:

> *Key Finding: A majority of organisations do not conduct regular evaluations of their PMO and also do not consistently measure benefits or returns from the PMO.*

> *... using a PMO contributes to improved project performance; however, organisations currently do not consistently evaluate and measure the success or returns on investment (ROI) of the PMO ... 29% of organisations never evaluate their PMO and 30% conduct evaluations on an annual basis. However, the 14% of organisations which evaluate their PMO on a monthly basis also measure their PMO for ROI (65% of the time). Those organisations that never evaluate their PMO measure their ROI only 9% of the time. Organisations can benefit from finding similar positive correlations between using a PMO and project performance, through conducting more regular evaluations of their PMO, as well as, business ROI.*

Measuring the PMO value will ensure that you are ready to articulate the true value of your PMO to the business as needed, it will also allow you to continuously improve the PMO's performance.

Lesson Four: Lock the Value in

The ESI report from 2015, *The Global State of the PMO*, identified that some 72 per cent of respondents reported that the value of their PMO was questioned by key stakeholders – usually senior management – over the last 12 months.

Despite one in three PMOs being managed at the level of the C-suite, it looked like PMOs were still struggling to prove that they add (or can add) value. Even after being in place for years, PMOs are still subject to scrutiny; one in three of the PMOs which were reported in the ESI survey to have closed this year were 5 years old, or older.

So maturity is not a safety net for PMOs.

The top reason cited in the survey for disbanding a PMO was that of corporate restructuring. On the positive side this restructuring could mean consolidating PMOs into a single enterprise model. On the negative side, though, an executive decision or change in management was cited as the reason why one in four PMOs were closed down, with an associated argument that PMOs did not deliver value.

The key here is that the value of the PMO should be 'locked-in during the delivery period and should be regularly re-assessed and continually measured by a good PMO leader.

It is critical for a PMO to achieve a level of maturity, as the *PM-Partners: PMO Trends 2012* report states:

> There's a direct link between the maturity of the PMO and the value it provides. Mature PMOs are far more likely to offer real competitive advantage to a business by increasing the speed and quality of business returns.

Lesson Five: Move with the Business

The *PM-Partners: PMO Trends 2012* report summarises this well:

It is generally accepted that the Project Management Office (PMO) typically defines and maintains the metrics, standards and repeatable practice for project management within an organisation and is the first step towards:

- *Increasing project, programme and portfolio success*
- *Strategy execution and business transformation*
- *Increasing the speed of time-to-market*
- *Visibility and cost control of execution on time and on budget*

Our survey results suggest that merely implementing a PMO in itself is not enough. The PMO must evolve over time with a continuous plan to mature the practices that are of the greatest value to executives. As a PMO matures and implements high value services such as portfolio management and resource management, the organisational success metrics improve, and the value of the PMO increases.

Regularly 'take the pulse' of your PMO and the view of that PMO by the business. If something has changed you may need to return to the business case and re-validated and/or update accordingly.

As detailed in *Leading Successful PMOs* you need to ask yourself and the PMO:

- Has anything significantly changed in the business that requires an adjustment by the PMO?
- What is the view, within the business, of the value of the PMO?
- Are there any key opponents to the PMO operation?
- Are the methods you have established well adopted and adhered to, and have recommended improvements been acted upon?
- Has the level of project maturity risen?
- Are project managers reporting the same issues as before?
- Has there been a change in the PMO sponsorship role(s); personnel or approach?
- Has project 'health' improved or stagnated?
- Is the PMO approach the right one?
- Is the PMO model the right one?

You may need to survey the PMO stakeholders to understand in more detail what it is that needs extra effort and focus. Alternatively, it may be that you just need to get together with your PMO team and revisit the PMO purpose.

Whatever the situation you must ensure that the PMO is in step with the current business needs.

Lesson Six: Connect to Strategy

For a PMO to successful in the long term it needs to be connected to the strategic activity of the organisation that it supports.

In the 2012 KPMG report *Business Unusual: Managing Projects as Usual* the importance of strategic connection for a project was explored:

> *Strategic Alignment: The success of a project ultimately depends on whether the initiative aligns with the strategic and financial goals of the organisation. It is, therefore, as important to do the right projects, as doing the projects right. 94 per cent of our respondents indicated that they have some sort of strategic IT roadmap that acts as a major input to their selection of projects. This possibly explains why organisations scored the maximum for this dimension; still a significant gap is seen between identifying the right projects, setting clear expectations and tracking benefits of the project.*

Pete Swan, Director PM-Partners group, declares:

> *A PMO is really adding value when it can adapt to the needs of the business and is viewed as a strategic asset during executive decision making.*

A PMO can operate at three levels of 'Strategic' maturity within an organisation, the first being the custodian of strategic intentions through the ownership of the projects themselves, each of which should in some way relate directly or indirectly to a strategic intention of the organisation.

This can be considered as 'Strategy Management' whereby the PMO acts as the governing and advisory body to the executive by:

- Validating that all projects that are initiated fit one or more strategic initiative;

- Tracking the current and valid alignment between projects and strategies;
- Making recommendations for 'stalls' and 'kills' for projects that no longer align with current business strategic thinking.

The second is 'Strategy Delivery' where the PMO translates the key strategic objectives into new projects to add to the existing portfolio (and perhaps to remove some from the portfolio if such objectives have changed). This 'Strategy Delivery' is supported by the 'Strategy Management' capability.

It may be that the PMO also takes some direct ownership for the execution of large and complex programmes (or projects) that are specifically critical to a key strategic initiative, such a relocation activity for example.

The final is 'Strategy Creation', this refers to having a role in helping organisations decide on which strategic options to pursue (and then to translate them in to projects – Strategy Delivery- and to manage their success – Strategy Management).

This is a rare situation that a PMO has reached this position of trust and influence inside an organisation but it is the potential future for the enterprise PMO that is successfully delivered and embedded with the right sponsorship within such an organisation.

In fact as observed in the *PM-Partners: PMO Trends 2012* report most PMOs don't even really 'get off the ground' when it comes to any of the three levels of strategic interaction or involvement:

> *The PMO trend is unmistakable, with over 90% of organisations surveyed having an active PMO. Over 96% have standard project management practices or methodologies, whilst only 47% have project portfolio management practices and methodologies. This is further reinforced by the fact that only 34% of PMOs are providing supply and demand planning, highlighting that there is significantly more focus on doing projects right than doing the right projects ... against a tough economic climate where the right investment decisions become more important than ever.*

Lesson Seven: Size Matters

It was interesting attending a PMO symposium and lecturing at a local university that the same question was raised in the space of a week – and that question was 'Is there a minimum size for a PMO?'

Thinking across the range of small-to-medium-sized companies then the answer has to be a resounding 'yes', partly because if you 'do' projects then a PMO is generally a good idea (what we mean by a PMO can mean many things to many organisations of course and we have to take that in to account). But also because if you only 'do' a few projects then when one comes along that demands significant investment from an organisation then the cost of failure is greater accordingly. A much larger organisation with a large project portfolio and equally large project community will be able to absorb and manage such a demanding project far more easily (and with reduced impact of failure).

So how small are we talking?

How about 'one'?

Can the sole project manager also be the whole PMO? Well, not really in truth – a sole project manager can't act like PMOs of many people since they can't act objectively with regards to their own project performance, they can't spend time investing in self-development and in method improvements and so on.

So not 'one' then.

Can a PMO be implemented in a small company that has limited resources, a small team of project managers only – perhaps two or three?

Well, perhaps not a 'PMO' as such but certainly a virtual equivalent with shared responsibility of some of the basic PMO functions that could be allocated to the remaining project resources – perhaps one person could focus on the training of project managers, another on method enhancements, and another on community aspects, etc. In this way a lot of PMO duties could be delivered to a reasonably high level.

Yes, I think a PMO can be applicable to all scales of project business but it might not be a permanent, dedicated unit of course, but more of a 'part time PMO'.

The biggest risk to such a PMO is the ability to offer the objective insight and support to all project managers, and the business. The smaller the team then the harder it may be to do this in a constructive, non-emotional, positive way – not everyone has the skill to do this and with a close team of peers it isn't always easy to do (or easy to receive at times).

Lesson Eight: You Do Not Have Infinite Capacity

The PMO is, if not here to stay, at least here for the foreseeable future, and more and more executives are supporting PMOs within their organisations.

The *PM Solutions State of the PMO 2012* reported that:

> *Most companies have a PMO (87%). Of the few that don't, 40% are looking to implement one within a year' which is great news for all of us champions of the PMO.*

The *ESI Global State of the PMO 2012* report stated:

> *The Project or Programme Management Office (PMO) has moved up the ranks in most organisations as more than just a warehouse of methodology, tools, and process. In an effort to impact business performance through training, methodology and project guidance, many PMOs seek to support project, programme and portfolio management in a more focused, strategic manner. Regardless of its particular position in a given organisation, the PMO is prevalent in virtually every industry and many governmental organisations.*

So this is all good news. *The PM Solutions* report also stated 'The greater the capability of the PMO, the greater the value the PMO contributes to the firm', which can also be considered good news.

Good news with a 'but'. There is a strong argument for a 'green' PMO to try and get as involved as possible inside the organisation but there are dangers in taking on too much. The PMO is well respected these days for the most part but there is also the risk that it is seen as a solution for everything that is not 'operational' and that it can deal with anything even loosely associated to project work.

For example, there are other pressure points inside the same organisations that now advocate PMOs such as the weakness that many experience in the area of executive sponsorship. The PMO can have a role here to act as a temporary sponsor, as well as a role of developing sponsorship capability internally. But that is extra work.

As another example many projects and programmes suffer from a lack of focus and resource in the area of Organisational Change Management. One large PMO ran a number of Health Checks in the most significant projects and a common issue found was in the area of OCM, with recognition of the importance and value of good OCM but with an equal lack of investment in this key area. The question then was is this a potential role for the PMO, associated as it is with projects and project success, or was this just a distraction too far?

In some businesses there is a renewed focus on good 'technical' capability to support project-based activity and the bringing together of these technical consultants in to one community. Some even refer to this community as a Technical Project Office (TMO), so should this TMO be linked with the PMO or should it come under the management of the PMO and be another skillset resource? Should the PMO remain 'pure' project management or spread itself across a wider community?

These are big and potentially distracting challenges within organisations, ones that a good PMO leader will be aware of and will have a voice to contribute to, but who will also have a mind to concentrate on the key PMO work that still needs to be done.

When your PMO is well established then consider these other matters but for now be wary of making your PMO a bottomless resource for anything and everything that the business pushes in your direction.

Lesson Nine: Make Things Better

Marissa Mayer, the new CEO of Yahoo, tasked with rescuing this once mighty company, has done many things in her first few months in charge including the creation of 'PB&J'.

A play on the 'peanut butter and jelly', much loved in the US, she's cut away ribbons of red tape and instituted an internal online service called 'PB&J' which actually stands for 'Process, Bureaucracy, and Jams'. This service allows employees to complain about organisational blockages and excessive overheads that slow action and decision-making.

It is critical that a successful PMO should be a 'balanced' PMO and this includes getting the balance right between people and process. Both are critical to project success and both come under the remit of the PMO.

But it is the responsibility of the PMO to 'make life better' for the people – the project managers, so that they can effectively and efficiently do their jobs – and for the business, so that the projects are seen to be under control and delivering benefits.

As you will have seen one of the critical tasks in setting up, or improving, a PMO is to review the method or framework that the organisation uses to guide their project managers. And in many cases it is often a need to add in quality reviews and some control points or stages to improve this control. But it is always a concern that anything added should add proportional value – quality assurance should deliver quality (and not be a burdensome universally hated overhead that delivers no real benefit to anyone).

One way to do this is to think carefully when you design such a process. The other is to make sure that you have a 'PB&J' in place for the PMO team to let you know when you have got it wrong.

Lesson Ten: Learn the Lessons

The question that is often asked amongst many of us in project management is 'Why didn't we learn from that experience?' and the same is true many times over when it comes to PMOs.

Albert Einstein said 'Insanity is doing the same thing over and over again and expecting different results.'

So why do we accept 'insanity' as the path of project management?

The next time you are in a meeting just try this out. Whether you are presenting or someone else it doesn't matter but what happens when the inevitable happens, you go to write something on the flipchart or the whiteboard and the pen is dry. How many of you (and the authors freely admit they are just as guilty) put the pen down on the rack again, pick up another one and carry on with the key, interesting, important point you were making? Thereby leaving the same dry pen for the next person – or worse, for yourself to do the same thing again a little later in the meeting.

Did you expect the pen to magically refill itself? Of course not – madness!

Did you put the pen in the bin and ensure that a new one was put in its place, or at least noted for someone that new pens were required? Of course not – madness!

A simple lesson in lessons learned, or the process of not learning to be more precise.

So are we programmed to not learn lessons?

Clearly not; if that was the case then we would have wiped ourselves out as a race a long, long time ago.

So why don't we learn lessons when it comes to project experiences?

Personally we do. Our personal project experience has to be a learning experience (even if that learning experience is 'I am getting out of project management and finding a real job to do ... ').

No, we do learn and we do progress and grow as project managers and we are all the better for it.

The challenge comes from sharing the knowledge of those lessons amongst others, and in learning from others experience in return. It is a matter of scale and capability all mixed in with time and priorities.

It is not the process of binning the empty pen and replacing the pen but in letting others know what and why you did that and how it can benefit them in the future and why they should also pass on this piece of knowledge.

It is less 'lessons learned' than 'lessons shared'.

It is a critical role of a PMO to make sure these lessons are both learned and shared in a practical way and to include the PMO members in that process as well.

So the next time you go to write something on the flipchart or the whiteboard and the pen is dry, stop – turn to face your audience and say 'Right this pen is going in the bin and let me tell you why ... '.

> **❝** All action results from thought, so it is thoughts that matter. **❞**

> Sai Baba

CHAPTER 12
Some Further Thoughts

Exactly where your PMO goes is very much down to you and your business but some of the current and significant 'PMO' related issues are covered here.

Monetising the PMO

A PMO costs! It is obvious; there is the money to staff and to run the PMO together with any incurred operational expenses and systems investments and, when the PMO interfaces with other parts of the organisation – as it should, there is associated cost to that time and effort. Of course the belief from those that sponsor a PMO is that the money and time invested will be more than saved by delivering more successful projects. And that is the primary purpose of any PMO, to deliver healthier and more successful projects appropriate to the business strategy of the organisation. Job done!

PMOs are not traditionally a profit centre and as such they don't generate revenue themselves, although it can be strongly argued that they do facilitate making money through the delivery of those more successful projects.

But there may come a time when there is pressure for the PMO to contribute more than that through:

- Partial cost recovery of the PMO.
- Cost neutralisation of the PMO.
- Profit contribution from PMO.

WHY?

If this moment arrives then you need to be very clear as to 'why' you are doing this (or being asked to do this)? If the answer is 'The PMO has been so successful we want to explore extending its remit to that of potential revenue generation' then that is a good reason. It offers the opportunity to calmly and objectively consider new ways that the PMO can work in order to achieve these new targets. It could be a very positive extension of the remit of the PMO and new stimulating challenges for the PMO team.

But if the reason is more along the lines of 'The PMO is too expensive and we need to save costs somehow so we either cut the budget or the PMO makes us some money' then I would suggest that you are on shaky ground immediately. The PMO will be placed under survival pressures and is unlikely to conduct itself well as it strives to make money, save money, and just keep going. This is an extremely negative and threatening situation for the PMO team.

WHEN?

The right time to ask the question of the PMO, 'Can you now make money?' and it comes with the caveat 'without impacting negatively on your current core work' is when the PMO is:

- accepted by the organisation;
- is stable in its structure;
- is mature in the services it offers;
- is connected to the business strategy.

Tick those off and it is OK to consider the next move. Your PMO can plan its extension of activities in to the money-generating world safe in the knowledge that it is on a strong solid platform and it is embedded in to the organisation. If you can't tick all of these off then the chances are you will end up 'fighting on two fronts', that is trying to build the PMO internally whilst stretching to win profitable business, and the chances are in this situation is that you will fail at both.

Let's now assume that you wish to monetise your PMO for all of the right reasons and that you are in the best possible position to do this.

HOW?

The best advice I can give here is the old advice of 'KIS(S)' – Keep it Simple (you know what the extra 'S' is for, I am sure).

What is your PMO good at? What have you developed, delivered, proven, packaged and can now offer without any additional investment or risk?

And what can be offered in a discrete way? The risk to any PMO of heading in the direction of money is that the 'customer is king' and this means that in any situation of conflict the money-generating customer of the PMO will win out over the budget-supporting sponsor of the PMO. So you need to avoid situations where the PMO can get dragged in to long engagements with 'customers' that distract from the core PMO activities.

WHAT?

What about Health Checks or Retrospectives/Lessons Learned services? These are discrete, potentially high value but (I hope in your PMO) well-proven packages of services that can be offered to external customers. Consider what else fits the bill:

- already proven practice;
- discrete in length of engagement;
- low risk;
- high value;
- offering some skill or experience that the 'customer' lacks.

Just take a look at your 'menu' of PMO service offerings and consider each one for potential revenue generation (if you don't have a 'menu' then ask yourself are you really ready for this move?). Once you have done this only focus on one or two; don't stretch yourself, but start easy. The organisation has to accept that the journey of the PMO from budget overhead to profit contribution is not an overnight one.

WHERE?

And finally where are these customers coming from?

If we are talking external customers to your organisation then anything that the PMO offers is going to have to align to and integrate with the existing sales and marketing and support channels.

If we are talking about costed services back in to the organisation internally then that has to be carefully planned and communicated. Other departments need to understand this plan and they need to build this in to future budgets. The worst situation a PMO can find itself in is to lose 'work' because they now charge for PM training, or project reviews, etc. As soon as the PMO becomes disconnected to the project business it loses any value it might have.

A PMO costs! And the first task of a new PMO is to prove the value of that investment through delivering (and tracking) improved project success. A second task it can take on is to offer revenue flow back in to the business, and that is quite possible but takes planning.

So how do you go about the monetising process, assuming that you have the solid foundations already discussed?

Well, this is a challenging one. I ran the question across 10 LinkedIn groups who focused on 'PMOs' and, whilst I normally find these groups and their members a very fertile source for comment and insight, the responses received were very meagre indeed and with little insight in to this area of PMO activity. Many people 'liked' the conversation but only a couple had any insight to share.

I take it from this that few PMOs have made the move in to the revenue generating world. Is that because it makes no sense to do this? Or is it because these PMOs are not yet mature enough to do so? Or perhaps it is just not seen as a sensible path for a PMO to follow?

Whilst PMOs are on the increase, as shown in many reports including *PMI®* *Pulse 2013* report, there are many PMOs that are challenged and immature and therefore do not pass the 'test' earlier described for considering moving to a profit centre.

HOW

But assuming you do wish to lead your PMO this way – I applied some thought to the approach, the 'how':

- Start small.
- Start focused.
- Start with a proof of concept and have a withdrawal plan ready – now if you are recruiting new head(s) to deliver this new initiative you need to consider what happens to them if it doesn't work out?
- Find the 'pain' – behind every service-based revenue earning opportunity there has to be a 'need' and behind that 'need' is a pain, something that the customer is willing to pay to 'go away' or to 'reduce the risk of happening'. You may well need to reach out to the other customer-facing teams to understand the areas that your PMO could service and then customise your offerings accordingly.

- Use your best and proven resources to deliver these new services and backfill the resulting PMO resource gap with new resource – less risk to your new PMO venture and better communication throughout with your 'proven' resource.
- Market what you offer – proactively 'sell' what you offer – develop proof points through 'success stories' – and then re-market, over and over again.

What business problem is the PMO going to help to solve?

There is proven wisdom in the advice that the PMO should only act on what is strategically important to the business and so the question has to be 'what is the strategic value in monetising the PMO?

- If the reason is to fund expansion of PMO activities internally – then this is a 'poor' reason.
- If the reason is to protect the PMO budget – then this is a 'bad' reason.
- But if the reason is to secure customer (external) project success (and new business in time) through the application of the PMO skillset and service offerings – then this could be a 'good' reason.

But bear in mind one risk to this move; the PMO operates for the most part in an objective manner, considering project approval, looking at risk, assessing status and applying guidance, etc., but in this instance the PMO would move to a more subjective role. You might consider some form of 'ring-fencing' of resources to reduce the risk of any conflict of interest occurring and to ensure that the PMO continues to offer the right guidance and authority in all matters.

Visibility of Purpose

One of the authors was recently on a panel of 'experts' at a project management conference and there was a great question from the audience about project quality.

After listening to some of the real experts on the panel he contributed something from his past experience and that was 'visibility of purpose'.

When acting as the head of a PMO he regularly ran reviews of projects and these reviews allowed the PMO to identify common issues that challenged the projects and one of these occurred on the larger projects.

On a large complex project (or programme) there would be many parties involved: the supplier, the subcontractors and third party partners. Then there would be the customer, the customers other suppliers, system integrators, consultants, contractors and many more. So what we always ended up with was a lot of people and therefore a lot of complicated communication as a result.

Now in the early days of the project, the acquisition period, it was typically a small team that worked closely with the customer and, all being well, would secure the business and therefore the project. There was then a kick off with all of the normal items on the agenda and from that point the project team would 'ramp up', i.e. get bigger over a period of time, and new people would join as time progressed.

Now to the point: it was discovered that in a number of cases as the PMO assessed the 'health' of the project a lot of the team members no longer (if in fact they had ever in the first place) understood what the project was aiming to deliver, up there, at the top or front end, at the business level.

So think of coders at an offshore subcontractor. Do they envisage for example that some small piece of code that they are writing to complete a piece of data transfer for the supplier, and therefore for the end customer, will contribute to a project that is targeted as reducing waiting lists in hospitals in the public sector? It is just an example but the point is that you would probably move through quite a few layers of the project structure before the project deliverables are directly associated with 'people' and in some way all project deliverables are about 'people'.

So the key is to try and ensure that 'visibility of purpose' is always at the forefront of every team member's thought, no matter what their role is, in order to keep the project focused on quality. Make it personal.

The PMO as Sponsor

In *Strategies for Project Sponsorship* (Management Concepts Press) the idea of what role the PMO could play in 'filling the sponsorship' gap currently prevalent in many, many organisations was explored.

'Is it possible that in an organisation with weak or limited project sponsor capability, the project management office (PMO) could act as a sponsor for smaller projects?' was asked, with the thought that 'It is surely better to do this rather than not use sponsors at all'. It was added that:

The PMO also might be a politically acceptable body to provide discrete support for project sponsors should it be required (and if, of course, the project sponsors acknowledge they need help). Because the PMO is the governing body for the organisation's project methodology and standards, it is natural that its duties would also include sponsorship tasks and deliverables. The PMO could easily and sensitively provide coaching and advice upon request.

The key sponsorship activities we explored to consider what ones might be suitable for a PMO to offer:

- Offering leadership for the project. This is possible as long as the PMO representative can operate in some form of objective silo from the rest of the PMO's project activity.
- Owning the business case. The PMO needs additional support, in part from a senior executive, to gain the right level of knowledge and independence from the business.
- Ensuring the project is aligned to the business strategy. This could be done as long as the PMO operates at the right level in the organisation (i.e., one that is aligned to and involved in the strategic planning activities) and is up-to-date with regard to the organisation's current strategic intention and thought.
- Governing the risk of the project. The PMO should be easily able to do this.
- Engaging and communicating with all stakeholders. This should be achievable as long as the PMO sits at the right level to interact with all stakeholders appropriately.
- Owning the realisation of benefits. This is a challenging one. If the PMO is focused on project success and the mechanics of project delivery and project management development, and more, this may be a step too far for the PMO.
- Offering assurance of success. The PMO can offer some degree of success assurance, but sometimes the executive may need to provide high-level assistance.
- Arbitrating as required for the good of the business. This is difficult if the arbitration involves management levels above that of the PMO's management.
- Overseeing the process of incorporating lessons learned back into the business. The PMO can and should play a key role here.

And from the project managers perspective the PMO may support the PM by:

- Being a decision-maker. The PMO can make decisions about project management support if the business grants it the authority to do so.
- Clarifying issues as required. The PMO must be in the know about the issue at hand to make clarifications.
- Resolving business issues that impact the project. It's unlikely that a PMO, however high up in the business, is going to be able to do this without additional executive support.
- Managing high-level relationships. The PMO can manage such relationships to a degree, as long as its management is mature and experienced. But there may be situations in which there is a need for high-level intervention from the executive.
- Helping with resourcing challenges. The PMO can assist with resourcing needs but will no doubt have to call upon the goodwill of business managers. Also, situations could arise in which there are major conflicts in resource prioritisation and a top-level decision is required.
- Supporting the project manager. This is a natural role for the PMO, as it is the de facto community of practice for the project managers of the organisation (e.g., looking after their training, skill development and certification).
- Applying objective comment and guidance. Though this is generally possible, there could be moments of internal conflict when the overall ownership of the PMO's portfolio of projects has to be considered over and above that of any individual project (or project manager).

It was further suggested that the PMO might support the project team by:

- Offering leadership of purpose. The PMO can provide such leadership if project team members hold it in high regard.
- Offering authority and representation of the business. The PMO will need to be backed by some senior executive or management body.
- Championing the project and help the teams understand the project's benefits to the organisation. The actual business side of the project should do this.

It was concluded that whilst some support can be offered by a mature PMO even the best-intentioned PMO cannot offer everything that a sponsor should provide.

But it was concluded that ' ... in the absence of a project sponsor, the PMO can fill a void. In this case, something is definitely better than nothing'.

The Rise of the CPO

We are in the age of the 'C' level executive, that is for sure. We are familiar with the terms CEO (Chief Executive Officer), and with COO (Chief Operating Officer), with CFO (Chief Financial Officer), and CIO (Chief Information Officer, although that one is not so old, despite its familiarity in today's organisations). We may also recognise CTO (Chief Technical Officer), but probably not CPO – that is, the Chief Projects Officer.

In *Leading Successful PMOs* Peter Taylor raised the issue of the 'C' level involvement in PMOs:

> *I have seen in the companies that I have worked for, and I am sure that you have all seen it as well, the special ones amongst us that are on a fast track up through the organisation destined for the hallowed ground of 'C' level appointment.*

> *And there is nothing wrong with that at all. They experience the company as broadly as possible with experiences in finance and in sales and in marketing and even sometimes in services perhaps. They get first-hand experience of the components of the businesses that will one day lead and this is a really valuable preparation. These are the one identified as having future leadership potential and any company will invest in such people for their joint futures.*

> *Sadly I have yet to see a future 'C' work their way through the project arena, the PMO, the project management practise. It seems as if, when it comes down to it, that the project side of the business (as opposed to the operational side of the business) is maybe a little less important, a little less attractive?*

> *So perhaps the 'C' is not immediately destined for the PMO leadership role but surely there is a critical need for such future leaders to understand the nature of their ever increasingly project based activities.*

Emerging from the growth in project-based activity and the importance that this has for organisations' survival and growth then the rise in PMOs is clearly noted but through this will come, the authors believe, the rise of the next 'C' level executive.

THE CPO – OR THE CHIEF PROJECTS OFFICER

The value proposition for this new executive role will be that such project activity is critically important to the delivery and achievement of business strategy and, as such, it needs to have a clear role leadership and have a place at the 'high table'.

> **"** Learn from yesterday, live for today, hope for tomorrow. The important thing is not to stop questioning. **"**

> Albert Einstein

CHAPTER 13
More Inspiration

If you have been confused by the various and varying reports on the 'health' of PMOs then one piece of recent news will re-confirm that PMOs will at least stay in the limelight for some time to come. PMI® have just announced that they now 'own' the PMO of the Year award programme. The PMI® website states:

> PM Solutions and PMI® have come to an agreement to transfer the PMO of the Year Award program to PMI® for the 2013 Award and beyond. The PMO of the Year Award is a perfect addition to PMI's prestigious group of professional awards, and opens exposure of the program to a much larger group.

> The PMO of the Year Award honors a PMO that has demonstrated superior organisational project management abilities by adding value to its organisation through its support of successful strategic initiatives. The award recognizes a PMO that has established a vision for value delivery and has had a positive and clear impact on business results.

This is a good award and, with one of this book's authors having submitted his own PMO in Siemens for the award back in 2010 (it didn't come in the top three but he still lays claim therefore to having led the fourth-best PMO in the world as a result of all other submissions being equal ...) we would urge PMO leaders and teams to consider entering for a future award.

And, we might add, for everyone to just check out the short winners' videos for some great insights in to other successful PMOs. Just search for 'PMO-of-the-Year-Award'.

Add to this mix PMI® now host the PMO Symposium in North America and you can see that PMOs are a hot topic for this organisation. And it is not just PMI®; back in the UK APM (the Association for Project Management) has formalised the inclusion of a special interest group for PMOs that had previously been an independent group for the last 10 years.

And the authors regularly speak at the other major PMO events around the world such as the European PMO Symposium and the PMO Summit in Rio de Janeiro and the APM PMOSIG in the UK as well as ESI's Centre of Excellence. This level of interest and focus has to be good news for PMOs around the world.

In addition to all of this excellent activity and opportunity to connect with other PMO leaders you can check out:

www.leadingsuccessfulpmos.com
http://www.axelos.com/officialsite.asp
www.esi-intl.co.uk/blogs/pmoperspectives
www.botinternational.com/thepmopodcast.htm

Maturity Models

Kerzner

Just like a physical from a doctor you trust, the Kerzner Project Management Maturity Assessment Tool diagnoses the health of project management in your organisation. It identifies strategic strengths and weaknesses and then creates a prescriptive action plan for improving the health of your PM efforts. It allows you to objectively assess your project management capabilities against key knowledge areas of the PMBOK® Guide. And it's all done online, which means it's easy for employees to access and execute. Scoring is automatic and instantaneous.

Developed by Dr. Harold Kerzner, the assessment framework is based on Dr. Kerzner's five-level project management maturity model. The tool has been industry-validated and is fully aligned with the PMBOK® Guide.

Employees who are invited to take the assessment answer a series of multiple-choice questions. There are a total of 183 questions, broken down by five levels of maturity. The resulting scores provide a candid look at project management within the subjective organisation. The tool also gives a professional analysis of the scores and offers specific suggestions for what the company needs to do differently than they are doing now.

The Kerzner Maturity Model is provided through the International Institute for Learning, Inc.

CMMI

Capability Maturity Model Integration (CMMI) is a process improvement training and certification programme and service administered and marketed by Carnegie Mellon University and required by many such as the US Department of Defense (DoD) and government programmes for government contracts, especially software development.

Carnegie Mellon University states that CMMI can be used to guide process improvement across a project, division, or an entire organisation. Under the

CMMI methodology, processes are rated according to their maturity levels, which are defined as: Initial, Repeatable, Defined, Quantitatively Managed and Optimising.

CMMI currently addresses three areas of interest:

- Product and service development: CMMI for Development (CMMI-DEV).
- Service establishment, management: CMMI for Services (CMMI-SVC).
- Product and service acquisition: CMMI for Acquisition (CMMI-ACQ).

The CMMI is a framework for business process improvement. In other words, it is a model for building process improvement systems. In the same way that models are used to guide thinking and analysis on how to build other things (algorithms, buildings, molecules), CMMI is used to build process improvement systems.

CMMI is supported in delivery by a global network of partners and consultancies.

OPM3

One of PMI's foundational standards, the Organisational Project Management Maturity Model (OPM3®) is a guide to achieving organisational project maturity. OPM3 is used to improve project processes, and increase and measure maturity against a comprehensive set of organisational best practices.

OPM3 covers the domains of Organisational Project Management, the systematic management of projects, programmes, and portfolios in alignment with the achievement of strategic goals. The three domains are Project Management, Programme Management and Portfolio Management.

OPM3 integrates these domains into one maturity model with three interlocking elements:

- Knowledge – learn about hundreds of Organisational Project Management (OPM) Best Practices.
- Assessment – evaluate an organisation's current capabilities and identify areas in need of improvement.
- Improvement – use the completed assessment to map out the steps needed to achieve performance improvement goals.

As with other PMI Inc. standards, OPM3's intent is not to be prescriptive by telling the user what improvements to make or how to make them. Rather, OPM3 provides guidelines regarding the kinds of things an organisation may do in order to achieve excellence in Organisational Project Management.

Consultants who are certified by PMI Inc. in OPM3 ProductSuite are trained to help organisations to identify and choose among improvement options based on strategic priorities, benefits, costs, technical prerequisites and other factors. In addition there is a Professional Certification available in order to work as an OPM3 consultant.

P3M3

The Portfolio, Programme and Project Management Maturity Model (P3M3®) described in this document is an enhanced version of the Project Management Maturity Model, which was itself based on the process maturity framework that evolved into the Software Engineering Institute's (SEI) Capability Maturity Model (CMM).

The P3M3 contains three models that enable independent assessment. There are no interdependencies between the models, so an organisation may be better at programme management than it is at project management, for example. The models are:

- Portfolio Management (PfM3).
- Programme Management (PgM3).
- Project Management (PjM3).

The Portfolio, Programme and Project Management Maturity Model (P3M3) is described by a five-level maturity framework. These levels constitute the structural components that comprise the P3M3.

- Level 1 – awareness of process.
- Level 2 – repeatable process.
- Level 3 – defined process.
- Level 4 – managed process.
- Level 5 – optimised process.

P3M3 is owned by Axelos, a new joint venture company, created by the Cabinet Office on behalf of Her Majesty's Government (HMG) in the United Kingdom and Capita plc to run the Best Management Practice portfolio, including the ITIL® and PRINCE2® professional standards. Their goal: to nurture best practice communities, both in the UK and on a truly worldwide scale, establishing an innovative and high-quality continuous learning and development destination that is co-designed by and co-created for those who use it.

p3m global

p3m
global

p3m global is a specialist project, programme and portfolio management consultancy focused on partnering with its clients to enhance their P3M capabilities to realise successful and sustainable change.

By assessing and benchmarking your P3M maturity and competence of your people, p3m global can create tailored improvement plans based around the training and education of your people and the enhancement of your processes and tools. Solutions range from helping you design, build and run your PMO to helping you deliver your projects and programmes in an environment of robust and effective governance.

p3m global provide:

- Accountable Delivery and Management of Client Projects.
- The broadest and most complete range of project, programme and portfolio management training and education solutions in the market.
- Assessment and benchmarking services for P3M competence and maturity.
- Objective audit, assurance and review services.
- Professional and practical consulting to enhance P3M governance and processes.
- PMO design, deployment and managed services.

p3m global are at the cutting edge of P3M thought leadership. We maintain and provide all leading global P3M accreditations to ensure we offer you a balanced solution and are at the forefront of authoring and contributing to many global standards.

p3m global is a PMI Global Registered Education Provider (REP) and Registered Consulting Provider (RCP), a Corporate Member of the Association for Project Management (APM) and an Accredited Training Organisation (ATO) for all British government endorsed products such as PRINCE2, MSP, P3O, MoP, MoV, MoR and ITIL.

Further Reading

Berger, L. and Berger, D. (eds) 2003. *The Talent Management Handbook.* New York: McGraw-Hill.

Hill, G.M. 2007. *The Complete Project Management Office Handbook*, 2nd edn. New York: Auerbach Publications.

Letavec, C.J. 2007. *The Program Management Office: Establishing, Managing and Growing the Value of a PMO.* Plantation, FL: J. Ross Publishing.

Perry, M.P. 2009. *Business Driven PMO Setup: Practical Insights, Techniques and Case Examples for Ensuring Success.* Brighton: Roundhouse Publishing.

Reiss, G., Anthony, M., Chapman, J., Leigh, G., Pyne, A. and Rayner, P. 2006. *Gower Handbook of Programme Management.* Aldershot: Gower.

Roden, A. and Roden, E. 2013. *Portfolio, Programme and Project Offices*, 2nd edn. London: The Stationary Office.

Taylor, P. 2011. *Leading Successful PMOs.* Farnham: Gower (also available in eBook format).

Tjahjana, L., Dwyer, P. and Habib, M. 2009. *The Program Management Office Advantage: A Powerful and Centralized Way for Organizations to Manage Projects.* New York: Amacom.

Turner, R. 2008. *Gower Handbook of Project Management*, 4th edn. Aldershot: Gower.

Some Useful PMO Blogs and Podcasts

And here are some useful links that will lead you on to more information about successful PMOs and some great insight in to what the world is thinking about PMOs right now:

APM PMO Special Interest Group
www.apm.org.uk/category/specific-interest-groups/pmo-sig

PMO Podcast with Mark Price Perry
www.botinternational.com/thepmopodcast.htm

PMI and Project Management Offices
www.pmi.org/Knowledge-Center/Knowledge-Shelf/Project-Management-Offices.aspx

Peter Taylor PMO leadership and development
www.leadingsuccessfulpmos.com

Glossary

Business Case
A business case captures the reasoning and justification for initiating a project.

Baseline Project Scope
Scope baseline is the approved project scope that is used to track variances against, such change requests.

Communication Plan
Communication plan documents the different types of stakeholder information needs, the frequency and format of the information distribution, and the method of communication along with the people responsible.

Solution and Design Document
Outline of the project, PMO solution together with a detailed design of that solution or solutions.

Gap Analysis
Difference from the current 'As-Is' status and the future state 'To-Be'.

Go/No Go Presentation
Formal presentation at each phase end to review progress and assess validity for progressing on to the next phase.

Health Check Report
Project assessment of.

Improvement Road Map
PMO enhancement actions and time frame.

Lessons Learned Report
End of project (programme) means to uncover, document and share lessons that can be uncovered for future project improvements.

Maturity Assessment Report
Is a descriptive model that allows PMO organisations to chart and improve their project maturity in line with industry benchmarks.

Organisation Change Plan
Organisational change is a structured approach for ensuring that changes are smoothly and successfully implemented to achieve lasting benefits.

PM Help Desk
Support team to aid project managers.

PM Methodology or Framework
Approved and standardised way of managing and delivering projects.

PM Methodology or Framework Effectiveness Survey
Assessment of adherence and suitability of the PM Methodology or Framework.

PM Process Guide
Process guide.

PM Template Library
Source of approved templates for project management (often as part of the project methodology).

PM Tools Report
List of tools available for project delivery (often as part of the project methodology).

PMO Assessment Report
Current state of productivity and performance of the PMO.

PMO Awareness Training
Training of the wider stakeholder community in the value and purpose of the PMO.

PMO Charter
Describes the purpose, background and objectives and services of a PMO.

PMO Manual
The 'how to' guide for PMO behaviour and activities.

PMO Marketing Plan
Plan of promotion of the PMO – its purpose and value as well as its successes.

PMO Organisation Chart
Structure, roles and responsibilities of the PMO (with an enterprise PMO this will be a hierarchy of multiple PMOs).

PMO Project KPIs
Key performance indicators to measure the PMO success/progress against.

PMO Road Map
Definition of future state of the PMO development with clear steps or phases to achieve this.

Project Charter
Describes the purpose, background and objectives and services of a project.

Project Closure Report
Formal end of project report describing achievements and next steps; it should be reviewed at final steering meeting and signed off by project committee.

Project Management Competency Assessment
Tool (sometime automated) to assess individual project managers' competence against a predefined skillset, used to measure achieve and to recommend improvements/training.

Project Team Organisation Chart
Graphical representation of the format of the project team.

RACI Matrix
RACI denotes Responsible, Accountable, Consulted and Informed, which are four parameters used in a matrix used in project decision-making.

Review and Feedback Process
The process of regularly (formally or informally) objectively reviewing the project progress or individual performance and providing constructive feedback.

Risks and Issues

A project Risk is something that may happen that might adversely affect a project timeline, budget, or scope. A project Issue is something that must be resolved/decided/designed or it will adversely affect a project timeline, budget or scope.

Stakeholder Map

A stakeholder is any person who can be positively or negatively impacted by, or cause an impact on – the project: the stakeholder map identifies such stakeholders to allow for a proactive management plan to be undertaken.

Training Plan

End-User, PMO staff, test resources plan for gaining the relevant skills to complete their tasks and roles.